Learning to Love the Peso

How to Move to Mexico and Why

Copyright 2012 Jeffrey R. Crimmel

Cover Design by Rita Toews

Contents

Prologue

Chapter 1   June 2010

Chapter 2   Why a Sunny Climate is Desirable

Chapter 3   How We Found The Baja

Chapter 4   Getting to Know Our Future Home

Chapter 5   What's Your Number?

Chapter 6   Snowbirds

Chapter 7   India, The Original Snow-Birds

Chapter 8   Transitions

Chapter 9	The Day After
Chapter 10	The Snowbirds Are Coming
Chapter 11	Winter in The Desert
Chapter 12	Getting Rid Of Stuff
Chapter 13	Ask a Lot of Questions
Chapter 14	The Move is Upon Us
Chapter 15	Here We Go
Chapter 16	The Border And All it Stands For
Chapter 17	We Made It
Chapter 18	Second Load To Mexico

Chapter 19	The Final Push
Chapter 20	Starting to Settle In
Chapter 21	Return for One Last Load Plus A Wife
Chapter 22	Overwhelm
Chapter 23	Finding Our Place
Chapter 24	Joining In
Chapter 25	Steve Forman
Chapter 26	Return Trip To California
Chapter 27	When Suzanne is Away I Will Play
Chapter 28	Everyone Has An Opinion

Chapter 29	What to do in July & Aug.
Chapter 30	Alternative Medicine
Chapter 31	Water Volleyball, The Summer Religion
Chapter 32	Continued Daily Life in Mexico
Chapter 33	Certain People Should Not Move to Mexico
Chapter 34	Exploring Baja And Beating the Heat
Chapter 35	The Great Southern Cal Blackout

Chapter 36	They're Baaack!
Chapter 37	We're Here For Now
Chapter 38	Why Did I Write This Book?
Chapter 39	The Last Word

About the Author

Acknowledgements

Glossary of Information   A to Z

Works Cited

Prologue

So! You're thinking of retirement and have heard stories about living in some exotic town in a foreign country. Friends who have traveled tell you how inexpensive places in Central America and Mexico are and there is even a maid to clean the house for almost nothing. For an added bonus Americans, Canadians and a few Brits are already living there.

Magazine publications at Barnes and Nobel are full of tales about investing in these countries. How does buying a house in a development with other Americans as your neighbors or having a home for your vacation and renting it out during the times you are not staying there sound? Does it seem too good to be true?

The stories are accurate when describing the inexpensive life styles and the beauty each community holds. The articles are usually from the perspective of the real estate person wanting to get you to invest, build a house or buy a home already finished. There are no descriptions about making the move and the hurdles one faces when transporting all your belongings to a development or town in a third world country.

Learning to Love the Peso is my tale of how I found my place in one of the many areas in Mexico where foreigners have moved to and changed their lives. An explanation of why I wanted to move south of the border and all the steps needed to make the transition are included throughout the book.

An historical perspective of why people move to warm climates in the winter is presented as well. The present day migrations made by thousands of persons who call themselves Snowbirds brings us the locations where people move in their attempt to avoid the winters of the North. Much of the information about the historical migration was discovered during my nine-year odyssey around the globe from 1970 to 1979. *Living Beneath the Radar* is my first book describing those adventures.

You will find the contents of this book helpful, and hopefully many of the views Americans have about third world cultures will be dispelled. Mexico especially is given a negative view as it is described in the news. The stories concentrate on the drug wars and killings in a few of the border towns along the Texas and Arizona borders. Many friends have told me how bad Mexico is. They say that living in a third-world country is not at all that great. When I ask them if they have ever visited Mexico, not to my surprise, most said no. They instead tell me about their local news channel where they heard these reports. Those who said they visited Mexico acknowledge their "port of entry" from their cruise ships either in Baja or the mainland. They never got further than the guided tours and souvenir shops waiting for them in their protected environment. This experience would compare to one taking a tour ship into San Francisco Bay, eating a meal at Fisherman's Wharf, buying a few sweatshirts for the grandkids back in Germany, getting back on board and sailing home. Can this person say they have seen America?

This book includes many stories describing the personal adventures encountered while making the move to Mexico and the adjustments after relocating. The information and experiences of this journey are written down within a day or two of them happening so the reader can join me in the adventure. *Learning to Love the Peso* is not just about the pleasant encounters during the transition. Filling in the gaps of the fun stuff, with the difficult obstacles as well, gives the reader the hard facts about such a move and the situations one has to navigate to make such a dramatic change happen. *Learning to Love the Peso* may increase your desire to make a metamorphosis in your lifestyle or completely wipe out any aspirations of living in the land of sunshine. Believe me such a move is not for everyone. Hang on and hold tight. **The journey begins.**

Chapter 1
June 2010

At the end of my first book, *Living Beneath the Radar,* my wife and I were going to be moving to Baja, Mexico when we were both retired. First we had to care for Alice, Suzanne's mother.

Suzanne was her mother's caretaker and managed all her affairs. Medications, doctor visits, filing her taxes and any other matters arising were just a few of the areas Suzanne had to deal with. Whatever was necessary to be done for a woman of 94 years, Suzanne carried out the duty. Alice was no longer capable of these tasks due to her age and the difficulties accompanying most elderly people. Caring for a parent is an involved, part-time job and it takes a lot of focus and energy to get these tasks completed.

We had moved to the Phoenix valley from Flagstaff after Suzanne retired in June of 2010. We moved her mother to Phoenix the month before and she now resides in a very nice home full of elderly people, many of whom have dementia. My first visit to the home was indeed an insight into a population not remembering the conversation they had with you ten minutes ago.

As I sat in the room, enjoying the air conditioning cooling me from the 90+ degrees outside, I was approached by different ladies in the home who were curious as to how I fit into their lives and why was I sitting in their home. I explained my connection with Alice in as much detail as I believed they needed to satisfy their curiosity. In about ten or fifteen minutes the same woman returned to where I was sitting and started the same inquiry all over again. The exact same questions would be asked and I would again give her my answers. I was visiting the world of *Groundhog Day*. The movie starring Bill Murray is about living the same day over and over again until the star gets his life right. I realized if I did not give all the information I wanted to share in the conversation the first time all I had to do was wait. The opportunity would present itself again in a matter of minutes when one of the ladies returned. This situation happened each time we visited the home where Alice lived and usually with the same woman.

Future visits taught me a little about the life of women in a home for the elderly. A lot of their daily routine is centered around the meals served in the main room. An hour before dinner the women started to appear in the main living room and found their seats on the couch and chairs near the dining table. Each of the ladies knew who sat where.

"Peggy sits on the end of the couch while Mildred likes to be at the table where she can snack on the cookies before dinner."

Routine is an important part of the ladies' lives in the home, and when a new arrival comes a bit of confusion exist for a few days until the new seating chart is established. Alice was the rookie. She took whatever location became available near the TV and dining table.

"Alice can have Sally's seat. She left us about three weeks ago and is not expected back."

I believe the reference to Sally leaving and not coming back meant 'she passed on'. I did not hear the words 'death' or 'died' used much. The women knew they were old and the "end" could be near for any of them soon. They were comfortable in the home they shared with each other not remembering what happened the day before or even ten minutes before.

Now you have a little background as to why we are still in Arizona at the time of this writing. I can now begin writing about the process of moving to Mexico from my perspective and maybe ease some of the fears held by some readers who also hold similar desires of visiting the nation to our south.

Chapter 2
Why A Sunny Climate is Desirable

The first thing one has to have before they ever think about moving to another country, especially Mexico, is the desire. In the latter part of 1973 and most of 1974 I was living in Amsterdam, Holland. I loved the Dutch and everything about that country. The one main factor stopping me from still living there happened in the early summer of 1974. Amsterdam, weather wise, can have great summers or terrible summers. In June of 1974 the weather was terrible which means the skies remained overcast all day due to the location of the city on the North Sea.

One day the sun came out and all of Amsterdam went into a ritual like I have never seen before. Long-sleeved shirts and sweaters came off. Tank tops and shorts were removed from chests labeled, "Do not open unless the sun is shining." People called in sick for work. Owners had to either run their own businesses or join in with the movement sweeping the city.

Walking along the canals that snake through this magnificently beautiful postcard-perfect city, people were preparing for their worship of the sun. Deck chairs were set up around tables on all the boathouses that lined the canals or on sidewalks or decks having access to the sun. Bathing suits that never saw the light of day during a cloudy summer were now in full view. Beer and drinks were set out with an abundance of bread and cheese, the staple food of the Dutch. Music could be heard everywhere. English tunes as well as a few Dutch songs poured out into the sunny afternoon. The Beatles and Stones were big in the early 70s. The party had begun.

In Amsterdam you do not need to know how to speak Dutch or even know the people to join in on the festival. I tried to learn Dutch for a few weeks but gave up when I found out that carpenters and common laborers could speak better English at a level higher than I could ever hope to learn from the Dutch classes. All I needed to do in order to join a group was to say "Hi" and start sharing where I was from and why was I living in Amsterdam. The Dutch are some of most friendly, liberal-minded people in the world. They are the most accepting of different cultures and beliefs of any nation I have come across. Now you see why I almost stayed in Amsterdam and lived there permanently.

The day continued with the sunshine-worshipping population remaining in the warm sun until it set in the west below the British Isles. The next day Amsterdam again woke to cloud-covered skies, the same weather we had experienced for the many weeks before. For me this presented as the norm for summers in Amsterdam. Everyone went back to work. Employers forgave the lame excuses from their employees knowing sun worshiping was just a part of what to expect in the city when the sun came out. The party was over and the summer clothing was carefully placed back into the trunks marked ''Do not open unless the sun is shining" with the hope they would again see the light of day before the month of October.

That night I went into a pub to get a beer and be around the Dutch who had just participated in one of the most magnificent citywide parties I had ever witnessed. After about an hour I heard a voice yell above the conversations and noise level of the bar.

"Isn't that interesting? Summer came on a Tuesday this year."

The laughter following the comment came with a few groans of realization. The statement could easily be true. I realized at that moment warm weather and sunny skies were not a part of the normal summer patterns. If I wanted to live in this special part of Europe I would have to accept this fact. The sun doesn't shine very much.

After having lived in Amsterdam for six months, Pavitra, who later became my first wife, arrived after visiting her mother who was living in Spain with her oldest daughter. I met Pavitra in India and we traveled together for a while and returned to the west in the fall of 1973.

Her mother was English and lived on a pension in Spain with her other daughter, Peggy. Norma, the mother of Pavitra and Peggy, could live quite well on her limited income in Spain.

This fact was probably the seed guiding me to think about where to live when I retired. Residing in a country where the dollar went further made good sense. I did not think about retiring in a foreign country again until after I married to Suzanne in 1992 and worked as a teacher in the Sonoma County School District in California. I realized the career I chose and loved to do was not going to provide me with a huge retirement in the future.

Chapter 3
How We Found the Baja

In 2005 our friends, Scott and Pam Anderson, took Suzanne and me on an exploratory trip to Mexico. Rocky Point (Puerto Peñasco) is a popular vacation spot for Arizona residents. Rocky Point is located on the Sea of Cortez and faces west so the sun sets over the strip of land coming down from California called Baja California.

Rocky Point was a town of interest for Pam. She spoke fluent Spanish and wanted a place to visit when Flagstaff was buried under two feet of snow and she needed a break from the cold weather. A two-hour drive to Phoenix is where many Flagstaff residents go in the winter to warm up. The idea of a place in Mexico only a few hours further that included a cultural experience, cheap living and a beach completed her desire to explore Mexico.

Gila Bend, Ajo and Sonoita became towns I would eventually hear more about in the coming years. They are on the way to Mexico. Gila Bend is located at a crossroad taking the driver either to Yuma and California on interstate 8 to the west, Tucson to the east, or Mexico to the south. Gila Bend is one of those towns that would attract a movie director who wanted to shoot some footage about strange places in the middle of nowhere.

The first thing the town did was post speed limit signs to force drivers to slow their vehicle to 35 mph as they drove either towards Phoenix, Yuma or Ajo. The residents in town want the traveler to really see what they have to offer in the way of desert oddities. A giant dinosaur, rattlesnake and a few other sculptures molded in plaster or metal decorate one gas station. Tourist items in the store found only in this unique town make the experience of getting gas unforgettable.

A little further to the south, if you are coming from Phoenix, is the Space Age Lodge and restaurant owned by Best Western. The 41bed motel offers comfortable sleeping quarters and a restaurant located beneath a Flying Saucer. The saucer is the size of a small tract home giving the location a one-of-a-kind look found only in a small desert community trying to attract customers. Families with kids do not have a chance of avoiding a meal at this place. Space aliens and the unknown from the stars never seems to go out of style with the younger generation. I have eaten there once and the booths were packed with families. The pictures and decorations on the walls give the hungry eaters visual entertainment while waiting for their orders of burgers and fries.

The Gila River is one of the main water canals in Arizona. The town was built where the river makes a ninety-degree turn. Thus the name Gila Bend came about. A few gas stations, pizza parlors, an Italian restaurant and different stores selling desert knickknacks found only in small communities like Gila Bend round out the offerings of this town with the strange name.

In 2010 a large solar company started developing a plant near the town. The sun is the only resource in the area other than tourism. The last time I passed through the town construction seemed to be happening on the north end of the road from Phoenix. With 1500 jobs needed for the plant, Gila Bend could go through a boom-period feeding, housing and entertaining the workers from the solar facility.

Scott, Pam, Suzanne and I headed to Rocky Point in February of 2005 when the grasp of winter was starting to loosen and warmer weather began to return to that corner of the world. Tiny border communities along the way provided gas and food.

The drive into Rocky Point eventually took us to one of the camping spots overrun by the giant RV population. These large homes-on-wheels were parked in two campsites allowing them to pop out the side rooms of their vehicles. The travelers set up awnings and got the cards out. Card games seemed to be the way many of these home on wheels residents passed the afternoons.

We looked like gypsies putting up our tents and securing them in the windy conditions, which seemed to dominate the weather. The town was a short drive from where we were camped and the beach could be reached with a short walk through the rows of the mobile homes. Our tents were among the few found in this Snowbird retreat and during our long weekend stay we found out a little about our neighbors and their lifestyle.

RVs usually travel in groups of two or more. That way there is always four players for bridge or any other game needing more than two players. Retired military men and their wives seemed to make up a large portion of the retired RV traveling community. This was evidenced by the bumper stickers and decals honoring the military branch they served. The communities seemed to be full of residents who knew each other and every night a party was held at some sight with drinking the main focus. I am sure Vietnam may have been brought up a few times during the fiesta. These vets were of the age group that war would have been their life-changing experience, saving America from the spread of Communism.

Several miles down the beach large hotels were either built or being built, giving the area a Miami or Honolulu coastal appearance. Fifteen stories seemed to top out the height limits. Every morning gangs of workers could be seen walking from the town along the beach towards their work of constructing more of the high-rise monsters. The long-range plan was to continue construction until the entire beach was full of these units. I knew I wanted no part of making Rocky Point a future retirement locale.

Our stay in Rocky Point included my purchasing a margarita set of glasses and pitcher colorfully decorated with a Mexican motif. Boats were out each morning bringing in shrimp, the number one catch of the area. Many restaurants served the grey crustaceans, which turn pink when served either in tacos, enchiladas, or on a plate of rice. The town is also a favorite of college students and provides a release from the educational grind. A few students still remained in town and we got to see them in action having breakfast. We watched several of them ordering a breakfast of pizza and a pitcher of beer at 10 a.m. This behavior had me wondering how many brain cells could be killed on spring break before the students returned to reading books and writing papers.

Nothing in Rocky Point presented us with desire towards making it a future place of residence. The one comment I heard over and over again from those who made this Mexican town a vacation destination was, "You should have seen it 20 years ago."

I assumed the comment had to do with the town being a quaint fishing village at one time before the commercialism arrived and started turning it into Puerto Vallarta of the north. The services for trash pick-up could not keep up with the demand and the main beach contained many overflowing basura (trash) cans from the previous week of the college population. Papers and other trash items decorated the gray sands. A good beach experience did not happen for us.

Another comment I have heard from those who visit Mexico regards the trash found everywhere. If Mexico could focus on the job of hauling away the waste left in the cans and develop a consciousness of not leaving piles of trash for long periods of time in public places, the images brought back to the States by those travelers to Mexico would be greatly improved. I understand the service for clean-up is nowhere near the level found in the country to the north. In tourist towns the extra expense to improve this one service could be a return in more revenues as visitors returned each year to spend their money.

At the end of February a Home Show is held in Flagstaff. The Andersons attended in 2005 and came across a booth at the show advertising another community in Mexico. This development was on the Baja California side of the Sea of Cortez about 100 miles south of the border from the state capital, Mexicali. Scott and

Pam were invited to an information dinner held in the Little America Hotel just off highway 40, which runs through Flagstaff. They invited me to join them in the dinner and slide show presentation to find out more about the newly developing community and the area where it is located. San Felipe is the closest town, located seven miles south of the development, which is called El Dorado Ranch. From the description of the area, I heard the town of San Felipe was now like Rocky Point twenty years ago. The town remained as a quaint fishing village and the prices for property were far below what was being asked in other Mexican communities found on the Pacific side of Baja or near the border of Arizona.

The year was 2005 and the economy of the U.S. and Mexico seemed to be in a boom period with investment in real estate out of control in both countries. The population of the States was buying properties with little or nothing down and hoping to sell and make a profit within six months. Poor money-lending practices contributed to the insanity taking place, and people were now expanding into Mexico with monies either made or hoped to make in the future when they sold such and such property at a profit.

The baby boomers, made up of those born on or after 1946, were starting to retire and many sought to get out of the cold of the northern states. Mexico offered an alternative to the prices starting to climb in the retirement states of Florida, Arizona, New Mexico, Nevada and California.

The presentation held interest for Pam, Scott and myself. We decided to take a tour on one of the school holidays coming up in the future, since we were all educators. Memorial day worked out the best for us and we arranged a meeting with one of the agents named Dan, who lived in Sedona. The weekly bus tours did not go down to the Ranch on Memorial Day weekend, due to the many travelers who went to the area on their own. The tours tried to avoid crowded conditions so those seeing the development for the first time would not be hindered by traffic or large numbers of people enjoying the beach and pool activities at the Ranch.

Suzanne stayed home for this trip. She remained the caretaker for her mother, Alice, who lived with us in 2005. On Friday before the Memorial Day weekend Scott and I met at the school where Pam worked. We loaded our weekend luggage into the large Ford Explorer and headed down the road towards Yuma where we planned to spend the night and travel to San Felipe and the Ranch the following day.

Traveling at night in Mexico is not recommended, even today, due to possible car problems and no one coming along to help. Cell phone coverage was non-existent in 2005 in the isolated stretches of the road between Mexicali and San Felipe.

The trip took us through Gila Bend again and then west on I-8 towards Yuma, located on the border of California and the banks of the Colorado River. Scott introduced me to Dateland, located between Gila Bend and Yuma. The date shakes, purchased by me many times over the next 6 years, became a routine drink and marked the halfway point to San Felipe when I lived in Flagstaff.

The location of Dateland would go through a major facelift in 2009. In 2005 the small restaurant, gift shop and date orchard located behind the buildings were the only physical things in the vast stretch of open desert on highway 8. Once I started to make Dateland a regular stop, I never missed an opportunity to suck large chunks of dates through a straw as I continued down the road either towards Yuma or

Phoenix. We arrived in Yuma and Motel 6 left the light on for us.

Denny's restaurant was a short walk from our room. Pam discovered Starbucks in the new shopping mall located a short distance from the Tom Bodett motel where we stayed. Starbucks was as important to Pam as it was to my wife, Suzanne. Every trip to Mexico from Flagstaff included a Dateland and Starbucks stop. The early morning breakfast at Denny's helped us get on the road quickly and cross the border at Mexicali by 9 a.m. We then wove through the capital of North Baja following the signs pointing to San Felipe and soon found highway 5 heading south towards the Sea of Cortez and the little fishing village 185 km away.

Bathrooms: The first thing I noticed in the drive through Mexicali was the number of Pemex gas stations found on every block in the city and several miles apart in the countryside. Pemex, owned by the Mexican government, controls the price of the fuel. Gas prices remain lower than in Arizona and are easily below the high cost of filling your car in California. The 400 billion plus industry makes Pemex the second largest industry in Latin America and only ¼ of the value is public investment. The gassing of your car is taken care of by an attendant just like it is in the state of Oregon. This practice provides a job for a Mexican citizen and keeps the business running smoothly. The establishments are kept clean and usually the bathrooms are the best ones to visit when traveling throughout Mexico.

Today, 2011, there is usually an OXXO store attached to the Pemex stations in Baja. The store maintains a clean atmosphere; provides coffee for the road and all the junk food a hungry traveler needs to make a long trip through Mexico.

The road to San Felipe in May of 2005 was going through the first steps of making it a major route to the beaches of Baja. Crews filling the countless potholes were working six days a week, but neglect could not overcome the many bumps we had on our first visit south. I now see why the many llantera or tire stores numbered more than Pemex stations. In 2005 highway 5 did not go all the way through and connect with highway 1, the road down the Pacific Coast of Baja. The paved road continued on to the small community of Puertecitos, 50 miles south of San Felipe. A four-wheel-drive vehicle or a two-wheel-drive car you did not care much about could only navigate the remaining dirt and sand road. The latter vehicle could end up as another roadside decoration abandoned and resting between two cardons (large cactus found in Baja).

We continued on past the farming and factory regions south of Mexicali and several communities along the road. Each of the towns included a Pemex and llantera store and eateries catering to the workers and Mexicali citizens getting out of town for the weekend. Soon the landscape changed with the road crossing several stretches of land having the appearance of dry lakebeds. I found out later the land used to be a part of the delta, connected to the Colorado River. Because so much of the river is used up before it reaches Mexico the delta is no longer in existence and only a trickle of water makes the complete journey into the Sea of Cortez.

Sections of the north to south coastal mountain range drop down from the main peaks. These mountains extend east to west towards the dry Colorado riverbed, like separate wings from the main body of a giant bird, resting on the dry sandy delta bottom. Several large sand dunes decorated the hills with pure white sand climbing almost to the top of these rugged hills. The road continued through three regions of the old delta, eventually turning back towards what used to be where the waters flowed from the Colorado to the Sea of Cortez.

Built on the side of the road near sharp curves are religious altars marking the crash sites of drivers who drove too fast for the road condition. The surviving families made sure their loved ones were remembered. The road straightened its' path down a coastal route. In the distance we started to see water, representing the northern reach of the Sea of Cortez. It first appeared as a mirage with only a thin blue line visible above a foreground of white. As we continued south the blue eventually widened and reached the beaches near the highway we were on.

Signs appeared along the road telling us of a military stop several kilometers ahead. The government of Mexico was doing their part in making sure weapons and illegal contraband was not being transported into or out of Baja. The check site location also marked the crossroad of highway 5 and highway 3. Federal highway 3 crossed over the coastal range from Ensenada and ended at the military checkpoint.

A brief conversation in Spanish asking where we were going was not a challenge for Pam. We were flagged on and soon the Sea of Cortez could be easily seen from the car as we neared the area where El Dorado Ranch was located just north of San Felipe.

Lack of a good sign marking the Ranch entrance caused us to pass the turnoff to the development and drive another five miles towards San Felipe. We turned around and found the correct road heading towards the main recreation area of the development with a pool, tennis courts and a restaurant located 200 meters from the beach.

We met our tour guide, Dan, and he joined us in a cool drink by the pool as he laid out our itinerary for our tour and stay. An evening drive to a Mexican hotel in town set us up for our weekend stay. Most of the rooms in the many hotels were filled with Memorial Day vacationers. Our hotel was no exception. The rooms were filled with Mexican families and screaming kids were still enjoying the pool during the warm evening. The holiday weekend seemed to attract large populations from both sides of the border wanting to be near an ocean and enjoy the small community of San Felipe before the summer heat set in.

For dinner we were on our own and we soon found our way to the boardwalk, called the Malecon, along the ocean. In Spain, Mexico, and Italy as well as some towns in Greece the population goes out at night and migrates towards the town square where vendors and restaurants are located. In San Felipe the same ritual takes place. On this Memorial Day weekend hundreds of families and couples were walking up and down the Malecon chatting and taking in the festive atmosphere as the cool breezes blew in off the large bay formed by the Sea of Cortez. All the restaurants were filled with visitors and locals. Eventually we found a beautiful restaurant on the waterfront called the Taco Factory. We waited a few minutes. Soon a waiter found us and started the process of ordering food.

Large drinks were served from the bar located in the center of the restaurant and we asked the waiter what they were. He said they were margaritas and each one came in a glass the size of a small washbasin. The expression, 'When in Rome do as the Romans do,' seemed appropriate at the time and soon we were sucking through a straw the largest and most potent drink I ever tried south of the border. Food soon followed. I always order chili rellenos when testing out a Mexican restaurant because I have found the best rellenos come from the best Mexican restaurants. The Taco Factory passed the test and we were soon filled with the food and drink from our first meal in San Felipe.

The Taco Factory where we had our first meal in San Felipe.

Mexican Hotels: After a short stroll along the Malecon with the rest of the visitors and residents walking off their evening dinners, we found our way back to the hotel and our rooms. A tip to the reader when staying in a Mexican hotel is this. Bring your own towel and soap. The top hotels supply the visitor with such items but we were in a basic hotel and I found myself air-drying after my shower, which did not include a small individually wrapped bar of soap anywhere in the room. The bed was comfortable and after the long day, topped off with a bowl of margarita, I slept soundly and awoke ready for the tour on Sunday.

Dan, our tour guide for the Ranch, met us on Sunday at the poolside where we discussed our lives as teachers and what we would like to see regarding the development. The Ranch was still in the infant stages of development in 2005 and the area set aside for the condos remained barren except for the four model units right along the sea wall facing the ocean. Trailers housed the real estate brokers' offices and were placed across from the pool and tennis court areas. A large building later completed in 2006 on the site was the Pavilion. It served as an all-purpose structure for a golf club, restaurant, meeting hall and party room where the Ranch celebrated the holiday events with the residents who already made the development their home.

The tour started with a look at the model condos right on the water. These units were as well made and beautifully decorated as any thing found in Scottsdale, Arizona or high-end condo developments in California. The views of the beach and ocean were magnificent and well worth the price tag, which was below any ocean-front properties found in California or Florida. A large open area was set aside for a future hotel to be built and most of the condo lots were within a short walk from the beach or golf course.

We looked at a few of the houses being built on the ocean side of the development and saw the beautiful tile work and styles of homes soon to be the residents of full time retirees or vacation homes for those still working in the States. The different home designs showed the creative side of the owners or builders who put together magnificent houses near the sea or the green fairways bordering the units east of highway 5.

The hillside development was another part of the Ranch located west of highway 5. Most of the housing construction I saw took place in this large area, which utilized seven different gated entrances leading to the properties being developed. We were shown several homes off of a road called Saltito, which contained the largest concentration of residences. A solar section existed on one side of the road and many of these residents had been there for many years, predating the present owner, Pat Butler, who purchased the development from the National Pen Company. Many of the solar homes had large open parking shelters made for RVs. The area attracted seasonal travelers for many years before Mr. Butler decided to create something special in the way of life style and recreation for residents of all economic levels.

Example of a mountainside home on the Ranch.

Dan showed us properties most of the morning in the hillside section of the Ranch. One area in particular attracted both the Andersons and myself. It was called Buena Vista. Good View is the translated name and it was located about 3 miles west of highway 5. The Sea of Cortez and the mountain range sticking out into the waters of the ocean separating the ranch from the town of San Felipe completed the views to the south and east. The surrounding mountain ranges that wrapped around the development valley provided the landscape to the north and west. Two properties, one street away from each other, were available and we soon found ourselves putting a down payment on future ownership in Mexico and a possible building site for a house. The view and location were so magnificent I knew my wife would also share my enthusiasm and vision of living in Mexico after we retired. This was my hope.

Our lot is to the left of the center house. What a view!

After one more night in the Mexican hotel we headed back to Flagstaff on Monday with another stop for a date shake and bathroom usage. Both Pam and Scott were excited about the prospect of owning a property in a development in Mexico and being neighbors with Suzanne and me. I was hoping Suzanne would be open to the idea of one day living in Mexico and still being close to the borders of California and Arizona.

Chapter 4
Getting to Know Our Future Home

Describing a place and showing pictures is not the same as actually seeing it. I knew we would have to visit the Ranch and give Suzanne a good look. Dan, the agent who sold us the property, had a unique offer for the clients he sold property to. He rented a house by the month on the Ranch but he only stayed there when he came down to give people tours. Dan used the house on Saturday and Sunday. If a client needed a place to stay and Dan was not going to be there, then the client could stay in the house for free. Suzanne and I planned to come down during the Christmas school holidays and get a feel for the Ranch. We were able to stay in the house for most of week because no tours were taking place during Christmas vacation. My two daughters were also coming down to join us and visit our future home.

The month of December finally arrived and we packed our bags for our first real stay in El Dorado. The drive down to the Ranch was difficult for Suzanne. Her lack of time spent in a third-world country made the experience somewhat intimidating. The poor condition of the sidewalks and roads in Mexicali plus the lack of build in maintenance and the poor living conditions in the countryside could really shock a new visitor to Mexico.

The biggest challenge for her was the number of dogs lying on the side of the road who did not make it across the night before. The previous night must have been a bad one for dogs because we counted five or six bodies beside the road. Suzanne kept saying a little prayer for each deceased animal as we drove by. By the time we reached the Ranch she was relieved and a bit shaken by the reality of death. There is a saying south of the border: "There are no stupid dogs in Mexico."

 I assume this means the dumb ones do not make it across the road and the smart ones learn how to cross the road safely.

We checked into a hotel for the first night because the house we would be living in for the rest of the week still had someone in it and they would be leaving the next day. My two daughters would be coming down the following day so we had a chance to explore the town and get a feel for the population of this quaint fishing village located on the Sea of Cortez. I was able to find the same restaurant, the Taco Factory, on the Malecon where I had my first meal with the

Andersons when we toured in the month of May. I believe dinner and the pleasant atmosphere right across from the bay helped Suzanne to see another side of Mexico and finally release the image of dead animals alongside the road.

We returned to the small hotel and settled in for the night. The morning came and we put on shorts and a light sweater to stop the morning chill. The daytime temps in December are usually in the mid 60's and nights can drop to the 40s during a cold snap, which brings frigid conditions all the way down from Canada. We were comfortable in our light clothing and did a little walking in the neighborhood before heading out to eat breakfast.

On my previous visit in May I remembered seeing metal workers near where we were staying. I needed a spot weld on a small shovel used to clean out the ashes from our wood stove back in Flagstaff. The head of the shovel had come off and I knew anyone of these metal workers could fix the problem easily. Armed with my forty word Spanish vocabulary and my lack of fear when it came to asking what I wanted, along with gestures and hand motions, I quickly found such a welder only a few doors down from the hotel. Two dollars for the weld and a dollar for the man who directed me to the welder and the shovel returned to its' useful condition ready to remove ash from our stove in freezing Flagstaff. I knew I needed to improve my Spanish to live in Mexico because I really wanted to talk to the local population and playing charades with them was not the answer.

The beach in front of the El Dorado development is a unique place. The large tidal change of 20 to 30 feet means a person at low tide could walk out onto the sand bar for about half a mile. They could collect seashells and more sand dollars than one could hold, either in the hat they purchased in town or a shopping bag converted into a beach junk-collecting apparatus. The first time we ventured out onto the low-tide sand bar was the morning after our arrival. We noticed several people with shovels and buckets digging in the sand and putting things in their containers. We soon discovered the large sand flat at low tide was a clam bed and many people were gathering a number of the shell creatures for dinner that night.

Suzanne and I collected about twenty sand dollars, barely putting a dent in massive deposit area of these round ocean shells. While we were walking back from edge of the water at the end of the sand bar I happened to look north. About two or three miles away a replay from the movie

'The Mummy' was taking place. A large billowing brown cloud of dust about 200 meters high was coming right at us. From the estimated fast speed it was traveling I felt we needed to step up our pace back to the car.

"Suzanne," I said. "This dust cloud coming at us looks serious. We need to quicken our pace and get to the car before we are blasted by the sand."

Suzanne did not want to be hurried off the beach. She was having such a wonderful time gathering souvenirs and other beach memories and the need to hurry meant she would loose time on the beach. When she looked up and also saw the brown cloud making its way down the delta of the Colorado River, she did quicken her pace.

By the time we reached the car the dust storm hit. We put the windows up and started the drive back to our hotel. We did so at a 10 mph pace following the taillights of the car in front of us also reduced to a slow speed. Visual sighting from the car allowed us to see only the white line next to our vehicle and the red lights of the car in front. We soon reached the hotel, locked ourselves in the room for the afternoon and made sure all windows were closed. A towel blocked the dust from getting under the doors. Several hours later Sukita and Kusum, my daughters, arrived. They retold their story of having to drive in the dust storm at the same slow speed we did in order to arrive safely at the hotel.

A few days later I met a man who was out on the sandbar with his family and a few other unsuspecting tourist collecting clams. They had not noticed the storm until it was too late. They were about 300 meters from the shore upon impact. They also lost their ability to see more than ten feet in front of themselves. The stranded group had to hold hands and trust the leader as he led the line of people to what was hoped to be the shore. Going the wrong way could lead to problems as the tide came in. They did get back to the car and survived the sandblasting they received from the storm and all its fury.

For the rest of the day and most of the next we were reduced to reading and staying in the hotel while the force of the storm continued. Long time residents said the gale was the worst they had seen in the past ten years. The weather finally cleared and we were able to move into the house on the Ranch. The other person staying at the house decided the storm was too much for her and she shortened her stay by one day. Along with reading, yoga and walks through the neighborhood viewing the many different homes rounded out the afternoon after the windstorm subsided. On the third day the girls wanted to do some exploring and the hot springs in the community south of San Felipe sparked our exploring interest.

Puertecitos is the small village located 50 miles south of San Felipe. Locals, living in the area, told me the town was populated by Americans back in the 60's when a large influx started to come down to Baja during vacations and school breaks. Rustic rock homes were built overlooking the Sea of Cortez. The drive south to the town also revealed another population of Americans and Canadians who built right on the beaches of the sea. Without power, solar energy was the only way to energize the fans and turn on the lights of these frontier homes. Dirt roads heading east towards the sea from highway 5 took the residents to their communities dotting the seashore. We stayed on the road south and did not visit the solar homes. Maybe on another trip I would visit these pioneer developments and see where many California hippies from the 60's ended up.

Driving in Baja: Suzanne remained at home while Sukita, Kusum and I grabbed our bathing suits and took off for the hot springs. The road to Puertecitos was in good shape and it seemed to have been paved in the past year because no potholes decorated the pavement. The only driving challenge on the road heading south seemed to be the many dips which allowed water to flow from the west to the east during the occasional rains in this part of Baja. At times a hurricane will swipe the southern tip of Baja and bring rains to the area in larger amounts. When this happens water runs across the road through these drainage dips coming down the many dry riverbeds flowing to the Sea of Cortez. It is probably advised not to drive in this area of Baja when rains are present.

The Cow Patty is a bar/restaurant just outside Puertecitos

The last part of the trip, two miles from Puertecitos, the paved road ended and gravel replaced the smooth ride. We were able to get into the town and located the parking lot near the hot springs after talking to a few locals who were walking around the village. A young Mexican man approached us and asked for a $5 parking fee. We paid the fee and found a place to change into our swimsuits. Paths led to the rocky area where the hot water came down from the hillside beneath the ground and out of the earth in small streams flowing into the ocean.

A few pools were filled with burning water and the high temperatures kept us from entering them. The only area were we could enjoy the hot springs happened a bit further towards the ocean. Several other bathers discovered one or two spots among the rocks where the hot water met the cold ocean water and allowed the bather to enjoy hot tub temperatures without becoming burnt. The timing of the high tide with the hot springs was important. Had we arrived half an hour earlier when the tidal ocean reached the hot water pools, the combination of the two water extremes would have allowed us to enjoy 110 degree bathing. I guessed the pools holding only the hot waters were closer to 150 degrees at the present, too warm for any life form I knew about.

After negotiating the rocks and finding the perfect location where the meeting of the cold and warm water took place, we decided to return to the local beach and get a bite to eat in a restaurant before heading back to the Ranch. A few people could be found sunbathing in the 70-degree winter temperatures on the beach. We were able to sit and relax enjoying our lunch and feel warm in the middle of winter. The return drive again took us over the many dips in the road and through the cardon forest of giant cactus plants beside the highway.

With the first exploring adventure under our belt we settled in and slowed down to the pace of the

Ranch and the "mañana" mentality we desired in our search for relaxation. Reading, meditation, walking and eating rounded out our days in the house. We took several shopping and lunch trips into town. By the time we were preparing to return to Flagstaff, Suzanne and I were starting to get a feel for the pace of life in this development and all the perks accompanying such a lifestyle.

The Ranch was still in its infant levels of growth. An example of this could be seen at the gates, which allowed the residents to access the roads leading either to their homes or lots where they planned to build. Bales of hay and cones used as roadblocks along with guards policing the cars driving into the development marked the many access gates into the Ranch. As long as the correct sticker was in place on the car window identifying a resident entry was possible.

When I took Suzanne and my daughters up to our property in Buena Vista we found many changes had taken place. A house near the completion state now appeared next to our lot as well as several other homes behind our lot and further down the street. The economy was doing well in 2005 and this was evident throughout Mexico. Large numbers of retirement and vacation homes were under construction where we lived.

For the next five years, Suzanne and I would come to the Ranch and get to know the residents living there full-time and learn more about how to make such a move in the future. Ed Jones owned the house where we stayed when we visited most of the time. He would later become one of my 'go to' guys as far as information gathering. Each year more improvements appeared on the Ranch development. Buildings replaced the bales of hay for the guard gates and this construction helped with security. The two main gates were completed and the road to the pool area was finished during this time. Many of the condos were built and most of the streets in this area were paved with brick. Landscaping was put in and the development was coming together in appearance and smoothness of operation.

Most of the condos were built by 2007

In 2007 I decided to get a real estate license and help the development send customers and possible landowners to come to El Dorado Ranch and at least have a look. I became an agent for the development through a broker located in Phoenix. At this time tours were still going down to the Ranch every weekend. I really liked El Dorado as a place to live in the future. The closeness to the States allowed those needing to buy items not available in San Felipe to shop and return in a day.

A medical clinic was built on the Ranch and the basic physical needs could be taken care of. Anyone needing major medical service could reach the States with a short drive to El Centro or Brawley. Helicopter insurance could be purchased cutting the drive time needed to get to the states. The big picture for the development was improving each year.

The year 2008 brought changes in communities throughout Mexico. The U.S. wars overseas needed large amounts of money to maintain them. The lack of regulation in the lending market for people borrowing large sums of money to buy homes and other real estate brought the American economy to its' knees. Some of the largest drops in the stock market happened during this year and the affect could be felt in Mexico as well. The numbers of people with extra money to spend dropped quickly. Soon the tours to Mexico reduced from every weekend to twice a month and eventually once a month. Mexico and developments throughout the country experienced a big drop in the number of those looking for vacation homes.

In the years following 2008 we still came to San Felipe and the Ranch usually during the Christmas break period. The number of homes being built reduced significantly and many of the local builders took the revenues they earned during the boom time and built hotels, building supply stores and started home-repair services. They needed to diversify in this slow, down market and even those Americans and Canadians who lived in the area full-time began local businesses to service the many residents living here.

Several restaurants offered American meals. Small stores sold items not found in the Mexican markets and a large sports bar with a pizza parlor opened during the years of 2008 to 2010. Mexico was also going through changes during this time period. Stores called OXXO opening everywhere. These businesses were built inside many of the Pemex gas stations or in neighborhoods. They sold many of the fast-food items and drinks found in the 7-11 stores throughout the U.S. They seemed to be attracting the money of the Mexican population due to the clean maintenance of the stores and a good variety of items not found in the mom-and-pop stores in small Mexican neighborhoods. Change was coming to Mexico. Adaptation to the economic environment appeared to be happening on both sides of the border.

If you get snow in October and November and
are tired of the cold, make a trip to Baja for a visit.

Chapter 5
What's Your Number?

When one starts to think about retirement, one starts to notice all the advertisements and commercials regarding this milestone. They are found on TV or radio. I was a pre-baby-boomer, (I missed the cut by 1 year) and advertisers knew there was a huge population also thinking about the same thing: retirement.

One commercial on television particularly fascinated me. It was by ING. The short advertisement used the phrase, "What's Your Number" and different people would be walking around with different blocks of numerals under their arm. These number signs were usually six digits long and sometimes seven. This number was meant to represent the amount of money the individual needed to have in order to feel comfortable when they retired. I would look at those numbers and say to myself,

"I do not think I am in the same number league as these people. There is no way a retired teacher is carrying around a number starting at 500,000 and going up to 1.5 million or more."

Other commercials focusing on retirement were those by Del Webb in the 60's. When I was a boy growing up in La Jolla I used to see the Del Webb Sun City commercials on TV all the time. Retirement became fashionable and Del Webb was way ahead of the game buying up cheap desert land and knowing one day the baby-boomers would be at the magical age of retirement. They would try to escape the cold, harsh winters of the northeast or wet, damp winters of the northwest. With a swimming pool a short walk away and several golf courses to choose from, sixty-five degree winters seemed like the perfect escape for those about to enter the slow-down part of their lives.

Being in the desert does not mean there is no water. There is water in the desert. It's just deep down underground or flowing past in the Colorado River after the winter snows have melted. The problem I see for places like Phoenix and Las Vegas is that they do not seem to think the water source will ever end. Developers and city managers continue to buy up farmland and desert, building malls and shopping centers and surrounding them with housing and retirement developments.

"Build it and they will come" seemed to be the mantra they used and it worked until late 2007. Beginning in 2008 the mantra became, "We built it but they stopped coming."

Many new homes and properties in states like Arizona and Nevada are empty, waiting for the economy to pick up again.

Soon after moving from Flagstaff to Peoria, Arizona in 2010, I needed to find a doctor. The computer again came to my rescue. It not only found a doctor for me in the Peoria area it also listed comments from other patients who rated their wait time, the doctor's attitude and any other subject the writer deemed important. The drive to the medical facility took me to an area of town I had never been before.

Phoenix is laced with freeways, main streets and secondary main roads going through residential areas without many traffic lights. I was driving down one of those secondary avenues called 91st street between Bell Road and Thunderbird on my way to the medical clinic. I love to see the different types of retirement compounds built since Del Webb made his mark in the 60's. On this particular drive I did find something out of the ordinary. I started to see canals and lakes filled with water and houses built right on the banks of these liquid wonderlands.

The development appeared as a mixture of Venice and Amsterdam without the centuries-old buildings lining the shore. This was Arizona-style canal and lake living with docks extending from the banks of the land into the water. Stone and stucco style homes and Spanish style tiles on all the roofs filled in the shoreline. Why move to the mountains and build on a lake? Developers in Arizona can build a lake or canal and place you in a house with your own rowboat or canoe to paddle around in when you want. I even heard the canals were stocked with fish.

If someone has the cash they can move into any type of living they want in Phoenix. If you are a Snowbird you just have to have somewhere else to go in the summer. Hibernating in the summer with the air-conditioning going full blast and a lot of books to read is the other alternative if you do stay from June through September. You only go out for food shopping or take refuge in the many movie theaters filling the city with 18 to 30 screens to chose from and the air conditioning going full blast. This may be the only time one needs a sweater during the summer. The air can get so frigid in theaters many catch colds from the two-hour exposure to the arctic conditions while watching Harry Potter battle "He Who Cannot be Named" or Leonardo getting into your dreams and robbing you blind.

Chapter 6
Snowbirds

Snowbird describes a certain type of human who seems to need to follow the migration path of other fair-weather friends who cannot stand the heat or the cold. Wikipedia says it best.

The term *Snowbird* is used to describe people from the U.S. Northeast, U.S. Midwest, or Canada who spend a large portion of winter in warmer locales such as California, Arizona, Florida, the Carolinas, or elsewhere along the Sunbelt region of the southern and southwest United States, Mexico areas of the Caribbean, and even as far away as Australia and New Zealand. It is also used for those who migrate to Victoria, British Columbia, Canada, for the winter. Victoria is known for having very mild winters by Canadian standards, and has an annual "blossom count" in mid-February to prove its warm winter status.

Snowbirds are typically retirees, and business owners who can afford to be away from home for long periods of time or have a second home in a warmer location. Some snowbirds carry their homes with them, as campers (mounted on bus or truck frames) or as boats following the east coast Intracoastal water way. It used to be that snowbirds were the wealthy maintaining several seasonal residences and shifting living locations with the seasons to avail themselves of the best time to be at each location.

Many of these *Snowbirds* also use their vacation time to declare permanent residency in low, or no tax states (where the taxes are sustained by

high tourism taxes), and claim lower non-resident income taxes in their home states. The right to vote for local office is governed by local law, so it may be possible to vote for local offices in both places if the locality permits nonresident voting, but representation in the United States federal Congress is for residents as enumerated by the decennial census.
Wikipedia

When I lived in Arizona in the Phoenix area and the winter migration of the Snowbirds population was evident throughout the state, businesses and restaurants boom. Roads become crowded, and movie theaters are at capacity during the earlier showing. When restaurants started serving 'Early Bird Specials' they were referring to the bird in the Wikipedia description. When the flocks head north in the summer, 30 to 40 percent of some neighborhood populations empty out and leave. They do not return until October.

Suzanne and I moved into one such neighborhood in June of 2010. Who moves to Phoenix in June? We did and it actually turned out to be a great move because no one is looking for a place to move to in Phoenix during the summer. The choices for a place are much more plentiful in the approaching summer months than in October, when the rest of the retirement world wants to be in Phoenix. Landlords are eager to get a tenant into a house for a year, so one can even negotiate a lease and get a good yearly rate versus a six to eight-month higher rent during the winter months.

The semi-gated community we found was located near the 101 and 83rd avenue in the community of Peoria. Everything we needed was within a short drive. QT gas, massage, manicure and pedicure businesses, Midas auto, baseball diamonds for the winter leagues, movie theaters and malls were available. Also just about every kind of restaurant imaginable was only a ten-minute drive to reach. Older men and women played golf every day on one of the two courses within the community. A center also existed for exercise including weights and several pools for either water aerobics or lap swimming existed. A restaurant and bar with several televisions enabled the older athlete to refresh himself after a grueling day on the greens and still keep up with the latest scores and games either in the NFL or NBA. This community was Disneyland for retirees, and we had a chance to experience it for a year.

After we moved in we started to notice the lack of people coming out of their houses either to place the trashcans or recycling containers on the curb for pick-up. A neighbor told me we just missed the going-away party the Snowbirds threw for themselves at the local community pool in May.

"But don't worry. You can catch the 'return from the north' party they throw for themselves in September."

It seemed to me Snowbirds are like those kids I went to school with who made life into a constant party. Party when you leave a place and party when you arrive at your destination. Party while you live at your summer home and party when you leave for your winter residence. Also party when you arrive at your winter home and, I am sure, many parties while you are at your October to May retreat. Not my lifestyle but for some it seemed to work.

On second thought, it sounds like a great opportunity for the medical community to set up liver transplant clinics in Florida, Arizona and any other warm Snowbird destination place. So many parties cannot be good for the sixty-five or older retirees no matter how many holes of golf they play during the week. As I continue to live in this community I am learning how to survive in the summer heat. I will document the art of summer living in a desert. It may come in handy at a future date.

When I was growing up in California we did not have Snowbirds, or at least not in the coastal areas where I lived. If you lived in Needles, California, that was a different matter. I think it gets hotter in Needles than it does in Phoenix. In the 60's only the independently wealthy were able to enjoy this life style of owning two homes. Many owned homes they traveled to when the weather got too hot or too cold and left their office managers or secretaries to run the business. If any problems arose, the good old phone company would have to be used to manage difficult situations.

My wealthy grandfather and his family (my mother, three sisters and a brother) owned a summer cabin in the Sierra Nevada mountain range. It was located near a mountain community called Camp Sierra. Summers in Fresno where they lived would get hot and a short drive was all it took to escape the valley temperatures of 100°+. Fresno is also a large agricultural area of California and the watering of grapes plus the nut and fig trees kept the humidity rather high and turned the dry heat into a wet sauna.

I spent several summers in Camp Sierra as a boy and loved this mountain community and all the types of people it attracted. Camp Sierra was a destination for church high school groups, which would come for a week and engage in their camp activities. They would pray, swim and return home full of energy and new connections with God and each other.

During this time in the late 50's and early 60's, young people, who dated one another at the Church camps in Camp Sierra showed up wearing the same shirts. These shirts came in bright colors with distinct patterns setting them apart from each other, so it was easy to tell which boy went with which girl. This fad did not last, at lease not in the San Diego area. When I reached the high school age no one wore the same shirt as his or her significant other. The garment industry was sorry to see this ritual go.

Each day I would go to the town store for something to eat or drink. The money I used for this special treat came from the glass bottles collected in the trashcans and picnic areas where people would leave them. A 3-cent deposit on glass bottles was a great incentive to collect and cash them in. We were the beginning generation of recycling. I am also a part of the eating-well generation, but when I was 11 years old that shift had not started. Fruit turnovers washed down by the soft drink of choice became my diet and reward for my recycling efforts.

While I sat on the porch of the local store eating and drinking my sugary snacks, I started to notice changes among the high school church groups. Couples were coming into the store but there was one main difference from the day they had stepped off the bus when they arrived at Camp Sierra. The shirts did not match. Couples changed being together and started to pair up with other boys or girls with a different non-matching shirt. As the bus loaded up with these bible camp teenagers at the end of the week, it became obvious, and the shirts told the story. High school romances do not always last. The summers I spent in Camp Sierra made this very evident.

Chapter 7
India, The Original Snowbirds

I believe the original Snowbirds migrating with the weather were the hunter and gatherers of any ancient clans and tribes of early man. I do not want to start quoting parts from *The Clan of the Cave Bear* so I will jump ahead thousands of years and begin with the ancient kingdoms of India. From all the literature I have read about this Asian continent of Rajas and other such rulers, these wealthy kings and queens owned a winter palace and a summer palace.

India can have some very extreme weather conditions. When the summer rains and heat arrived the rulers would pack up their 200 wives, with all their needs and head to the summer palace. With Raja wives I am sure there would be a lot of luggage to transport. These great migrations either to the Himalayan foothills or to the Eastern and Western Ghats, depending upon where their kingdom was located, would be a sight to see.

The Ghats are higher mountain ranges running down the eastern and western sides of India. Many of the servants and workers helping to fill the needs of such rulers and all their wives would also get to go and enjoy the wonderful temperate weather conditions of the higher elevations. Any rulers with a kingdom only in the Rajasthan Desert were out of luck. The servants operating the fans had to work extra hard during the summer season.

The opposite migrations occurred when winter approached and the kingdoms headed down to the lower elevations and the warmer conditions awaiting them. Once settled in for the winter, with all the fans packed away and the winter clothing brought out, the kings would again start to govern their people and make sure they were safe from attack from other jealous rulers not having a summer palace like they did. If a ruler lives near the Rajasthan desert he better have a strong army to hold back those hot desert people who had to stay all summer in the heat. By July or August they could be super-agitated from the heat and ready to conquer a neighbor with a portion of cooler elevations within their borders.

The English also took over the idea of summer homes from the Rajas and rulers of India when they conquered this region and ruled it for over 400 years. Darjeeling is a hill station in the foothills of the Himalayan Mountains built for the wealthy English generals and businessmen who ran India. The buildings and homes are the style one would find in England. Remember, only the wealthy were able to escape the heat of summer in India and the lower ranked officers and clerks remained in the lowland and kept India running. They survived beneath revolving fans moving only the hot air around in the room, giving the impression there was a breeze blowing.

While living in India in the 70s I visited several hill communities including Darjeeling, Manali, and Dalhousie. Many of these towns still have the English-style architecture either surrounding a town square or beautiful homes located near the towns. Because the elevation ranged from 7000 ft. to 9000 ft. the homes and some businesses were closed in the winter and remained so during the extreme conditions of cool weather brought on by the Himalayan Mountains just to the north. As soon as the snows melted and the valley temperatures began to climb, the owners would return to their stores and homes and conduct business serving the many travelers escaping the heat from the Indian plains.

Suzanne and I are like those lower-ranked officers who got left behind. We just moved to Phoenix and are just now learning how to survive the condition of 115 degrees Fahrenheit in a place where only roadrunners and rattlesnakes call this desert home. The brief walks from air-conditioned cars to air-conditioned buildings, with the blast of heat in-between, is enough to sap your energy for the day. Those who have lived in this town for a while say they have become used to it but I do not know if that is really possible. My blood was still on the thick side after living for ten years in Flagstaff where the temperatures rarely reached more than the high 80s in the middle of summer.

Where I grew up in San Diego the weather stays fairly temperate all year, especially along the coast. I lived in La Jolla, so the ocean fog in the early mornings of summer cooled things down and the warm ocean in the winter did not allow the temperature to drop much below 60 degrees. This reason alone is also why so many people, wanting a livable climate all year round, moved to Southern California. It is also why the original families who grew up along these beautiful coastal towns cannot afford to live there any longer due to the demand and higher prices for everything. The only people I knew from La Jolla who still live there either became doctors or took over their parents' real estate businesses. An agent can live quite well from the sale of a few houses each year in La Jolla.

Chapter 8
Transitions

August 1, 2010. It has been raining all day and the temperature has not risen above 85 degrees. This may not be an unusual weather report for most of the country but for Phoenix, Arizona in the summer, it is strange. This is also the day that Suzanne's mother passed. It happened around five o'clock in the morning. She had a stroke on the previous Monday and was in a coma for three days. Luisa, her daughter who lives in New York, flew out. She was close to her mother, and Suzanne and I knew the passing would be hard on her.

On Thursday, Alice came out of the coma. She could not communicate too well and she had not eaten or had any liquids at all during this period. She was on hospice care, and the focus was to keep her comfortable and as pain-free as possible. She was also 94 and weighed between 75 and 80 pounds, and we all knew the time was near for her to make her transition. The caretaker asked her if she was hungry. She understood him and said "yes" but all she could eat was ice cream. She could not take any liquids and anything solid was also not possible.

This next statement is not meant to be disrespectful. Ben and Jerry, I have a new name for a flavor you need to invent. It's called 'The Last Bite.' Many older people during their last days on earth cannot eat solid foods. What a great way to celebrate one's life by having ice cream as your last meal. Just make sure the new flavor does not have nuts or fruit. It must be smooth in order to go down easily.

Alice came out of the coma and it seemed she did so for Luisa. Both Suzanne and Luisa were with her on Friday and Saturday but she was not able to sustain being awake long and would slip back into her sleep-state after a few bites of ice cream. The visits were not long and only a few words would pass between the daughters and their mother.

On Sunday morning Suzanne got a call saying Alice had passed. We quickly dressed and went to the home to say our last good-bys to Alice before hospice and the Nautilus Foundation came to remove her body. From that moment on the day seems to have shifted gears for Suzanne and me. Everything started to move in slow motion. I went to get gas and coffee after dropping the two sisters off with their mother. The world was operating at its usual pace but I was moving slowly, or should I say going below the speed limit. I got gas for the car and coffee for Suzanne and myself. I returned just as the Nautilus Foundation van was pulling away and taking the body for cremation.

Suzanne has been caring for her mother for 10+ years. She is now in a state of relief and sadness. She did a great job doing all the taxes, doctor visits, medication ordering, and many others tasks needed for a parent who cannot do them. About six months ago her mother asked Suzanne, "Am I your mother or are you my mother?"

Alice had first stage dementia but she knew who we were. When a parent goes through the process of aging and approaching the end of life, it seems the roles become reversed and the parent feel like the child being cared for and the daughter feels like the parent caring for the child. The husband has a role in this too. Support what your wife is doing because she needs backup to see the process through.

Suzanne sat on the couch with me. I had just finished reading the book *Eat, Pray, Love.* I have been to all those places in Gilbert's book and I was married to my first wife on Bali in 1975. Our minds were racing. We started to rethink retirement. We thought we could also go to South America, Nepal, Bali and any other place and live for a while until we wanted to move to our first place of choice at El Dorado Ranch in Baja Californa. I think we are going through a 'rethink about life' phase because our future has just changed with the passing of Alice. We really do not know at this moment what we really want to do. This is probably how transitions affect those left behind.

I told you I was going to write this book in the here and now and I am 'Here' and this is 'Now.'

Chapter 9
The Day After

I tried to go to work on Monday and at the same time I knew I was still floating through in a time warp a day after Alice passed. I had taken an aide job at a charter school. After retiring from teaching I knew I was going to work in some capacity and I think I stayed with education because it is never boring. The days go by quickly and I still have time to write in the mornings. I also actually like most kids and my two years with a charter school in Flagstaff allowed me to be around young adults who really wanted to learn and who came from families who supported them in their education needs.

After an hour and a half of introductions at the charter school where I was hired and new information was presented as to how the school was going to change, I went to the principal and told him what had happened to my mother in law. I needed to help remove her belongings from the home she had stayed. He had just lost his mother recently and he knew what I was going through. He told me to take the rest of the day off and deal with the moving chore. I agreed and drove home. Around 10 A.M. it hit me. My energy was sapped and I still had a lot to do.

I arrived home. I picked up Suzanne and Luisa in the car and returned to the house where Alice had lived. She had died the day before but it seemed like last week. Time was really messing with us and the world still seemed to go by at a much faster pace than Suzanne or I were experiencing. We were still in the slow lane going 45 and everyone else maintained a speed of 65 or faster.

The chore of picking up the furniture was completed and we returned home after having lunch in a bread-and-soup place called Paradise Bakery, which emphasized healthy eating with a chocolate cookie for desert. I have to admit the cookie tasted really great and the sugar helped me get the car home without nodding out at the wheel.

Today is day two of my return to school. I will see how this new job plays out.

The morning sessions of the school where I have taken an aide position was filled with the owner telling his story as to how he became interested in starting and owning charter schools. He owns two of them. They started with his mother, who did not like the reading curriculum in the Mesa school district. She tried many times along with plenty of parent support to get the district to change what they read. Each time they were rebuked and told, "We are the educators. Relax and let us do our job."

When it comes to reading matter I have to agree with parents who are involved with the education of their children. I do not believe educators have all the answers and at the same time neither do the parents. If parents do not like something about a school and what they represent and they are in a minority, then they have the choice to search for another school or start their own. This is what the owner of the school did. His parents did not care for the public school curriculum and they found out how to start their own school. They were the first to make start a charter in the area and this is how the birth of alternative schools in Phoenix began.

I am now at the end of the first week at the school. Fundamentalism and conservative political views seems to make up the majority of the teaching population. Can I remain under the radar and not raise my political head and voice my stance? Surrounded by people with a completely different philosophy as to how they see the world is like being in a foreign country and not understanding the language. Rush Limbaugh is an extreme right-wing radio personality. The son of the owner of the school was a follower of his views. After he quoted a Limbaugh statement at the school one day, I looked around the lunch room and saw no one objecting to the rhetoric coming from the lips of this man who made Rush his guru. I knew I was not in Kansas any more.

America is becoming isolated in many ways, and this direction we are taking is building the wall of separation from America and other cultures. The wall is so high we can no longer see their points of view. This is a path to implosion, and this is completely the opposite of what this country stood for when we raised the Statue of Liberty: "Give me your tired, your poor, your hungry masses yearning to be free."

Our country now has a political party that is trying to delete the 14th Amendment to our constitution. It states:

"The Fourteenth Amendment to the United States Constitution, which grants citizenship to all people born in the US (and subject to the jurisdiction thereof) and prohibits individual states from infringing on civil and political rights."

This scenario reminds me of the famous quote from Pogo. "We have met the enemy and he is us."

You may think this is pretty harsh criticism for someone who is writing a book catering to a retirement community. Many may hold conservative views but here is my thought. Anyone who wants to retire in a third-world foreign country probably does not have a fear-based ideological understanding of what they think the world is like. They have probably traveled and experienced different cultures in their lifetime. They probably believe people of color are thinking people like themselves with the same worries and concerns. I would not like a person living with me in Mexico spewing negative comments about the locals in town or those working for the Ranch in some capacity.

It has now been a month since starting work at the conservative charter school in Peoria and I am about to become a substitute teacher instead. It has been a difficult transition becoming an aide for a first year teacher who is completely overwhelmed working with 18 children, 13 of whom are ADD and completely out of control by the afternoon due to their meds wearing off. I am there for 8 hours and by the time I get home I am completely shot, having done outside duty in 98 to 110 degree weather and drinking my weight in water during the day. (That's a lot of water.)

I handed out cards about my travel book to a couple of teachers. They looked up the web page and read on the back cover about my life experiences. Meeting a Buddhist nun after she was sealed in a cave for 6 years practicing meditation and my visit to Islamic Mosques where God is worshiped became too much. The beginning of the end for my stay at the charter school was near.

By Thursday of the following week I was called into the principal's office and told by the head master that the school needed to make some aide adjustments and my services were no longer needed. I was relieved because I did not have to make any physical excuses to the principal as to why I could no longer work at the school. A big weight has been taken off my shoulders. I now understand why the contracts for the aides contained a clause that said the school could terminate the person at any time for no reason and I could also quit at any time for no reason. I am not a fundamentalist Christian. They could not have any person work at their fundamental Christian school disguised as a charter school getting public funds from the state of Arizona and not share their same beliefs. I might say something to a child contrary to their way of thinking and this would be a disaster. Wow! I was glad to leave that school.

Chapter 10
The Snow Birds Are Coming

It is now the middle of September in Peoria, AZ. The seasons are starting to change. When you live in a desert community the changes are very subtle. The temperatures are still in the 100s but occasionally a cool spell happens and the low 90s are the high for the day and the evenings drop to 70 degrees. During the cooler evenings I see the local Phoenix population starting to put on light sweaters and pull out their jeans in preparation for the winter where nights drop to the 40s and 50s and the days only reach the 60s or low 70s.

We are awaiting the migration of the "Snowbirds" who make their yearly return to the desert from their summer homes in Canada and the cooler northern states. You don't need a pair of binoculars to see this kind of bird. What you need to do is get into a party mood because these birds usually have welcome-back gatherings at all the local community pools throughout the development. Celebrating the 60 and 70-degree winter weather in Phoenix can be enough reason to feel good about life.

I saw a bumper sticker on a car the other day. It read something like this: "Open season on Snowbirds" The problem I have with such a statement has to do with the local economies. Those who cater to these winter residents increase their income in every respect. The winter residents are a big plus to the Phoenix economy. Do not bite the hand that feeds you.

Another point I would like to make regarding those who stay for the summer and those who leave is this. Many of the semi-retired or retired actually still work full or part-time. Many of the fully retired are in such a poor level of physical health they cannot travel to a cooler region. They hibernate in their homes for the summer.

During the peak heat I rarely saw any neighbors outside of their homes. An exception would be the early evening dip in the pools to cool down from the 114-degree days while floating in the 92-degree water. Agua at that temperature was actually refreshing. The air was still in the upper 90s or higher and the cooler water did lower the body heat and made the evenings at home more enjoyable.

Chapter 11
Winter in the Desert

We have just survived a winter in the Phoenix, the desert capital of Arizona. We managed to get through 60-degree days in the dead of winter while watching the weather reports on the news showing how the east coast survived during December and January of 2010 and 2011. I see why people come here from all the cold areas of the country. They board up their houses in the north and run around in shorts and tee shirts from October to May. Right now the Canadians are preparing to return to their northern homes because they have to live at least 6 months in their country to still receive the health and retirement benefits. They do not want any part of the health plan in the States because it costs too much. Canada has a national health plan for all residents.

Medications: This past month a health advisor told me about the mail-service drug companies in Canada who ship generic medications to many people in the States. I was just about to go into the *donut hole* and pay $300 for my last medication of the year instead of 60 bucks for a three-month's supply. Almost all medications are made in generic form and distributed through Canadian suppliers. The *donut hole* is a term used to describe when the Medicare Insurance for prescription drugs is used up. The individual then has to pay the outrageous high prices the drug companies charge for their medications.

A good way to save on medications is using this plan. Have your doctor prescribe a double strength amount of a drug. When they arrive cut them in half. My doctor in Peoria had no problem doing this. I take 20 mg of Benicar. The medication would cost me $120 for a three-month's supply because AARP no longer offers the $60 plan for three-months. I now get three-months of the generic form in 40mg tablets for $85. I cut the tabs in half so it last for 6 months. The cost is $170 for the year vs. Plan D through

AARP for $480. I have been tested since taking the generic drugs and all my tests are normal. There is no *donut hole* and I get the drugs in the mail just like I did before. I have to give the mailing period about four weeks vs. 10 days with AARP so I just plan ahead.

I priced the drugs in San Felipe at drug stores and they are not as good as the price of the generic medications from Canada. Here are the names of the Canadian generic drug companies: Global Pharmacy Canada with the customer service number 866-850-6021 is the first company I used. I now use Global Drug Supply, which works with Canada Drugs, and their number is 800-226-3784. I switched to them because they are located in the middle of Canada and closer to where I live. One of the medications I used from the other Canadian company was cheaper and Global Drug Supply has a policy of matching any other drug company's price if the other manufacturer has less expensive medications.

If you are interested in this approach to obtaining your medications then give each company a call and receive a price list. Prices are also available on line. Usually a good American doctor will prescribe a double dose of medication for you when he hears the story of how you want to save on generic medications, and can do so by cutting the medications in half. Pill cutters are available in pharmacy stores. Have yourself tested after a few weeks of taking the generic medication to make sure they are working for you. I have done so and have found the generic medications do the job quite well at a fraction of the price. After you read this page rip it out of the book and burn it. I do not want the American drug companies coming after me for passing on money-saving tips to the public and cutting into their billion-dollar profits.

This is an additional update on drugs. I have been comparing the prices of the medications in the border town near Yuma, Arizona called Algodones. The generic form of Lipitor is the same price as the Canadian generic form. Also a few of my medications are a little cheaper. If the reader is close to Algodones they can park on the U.S. side, cross the border, shop, have lunch and see what your medication costs. The Canadian prices are a good alternative if Mexico is too far away.

Chapter 12
Getting Rid of Stuff

It is now April and we are making the first move to lessen our load of items for our house in Baja,

Mexico. My daughter, Kusum, is coming by on Monday to collect the antique furniture given to me by my mother. She lives in the Bay Area and Victorian furniture in California instead of Mexico is a much better fit. Suzanne is moving her antique furniture and other items we will not need in Mexico to her brother's house. Michael just bought a house from a bank sale outside Phoenix. The depleted real estate market has allowed those who are house-shopping to get some really great deals in this devastated market. After Suzanne's furniture is gone we will be reduced to a bed, three tables, chairs, kitchen items and books. Along with the files and other items needed to live in Mexico, we have little to move. Mexican furniture will be purchased once we are settled in.

I noticed something on our last visit to Baja, which may be of interest to the reader. The Mexican people have come up with ways to accommodate the needs of North Americans and Canadians who move there and still want the same connections for phone, television and Internet as in the States. I also have noticed certain stores are stocking up with organic and healthier food items Americans have become used to. Rice milk and soy products are just a few of the many organic items appearing in certain stores.

Where I am moving in Mexico is only a day trip to El Centro and back. Going on a food run at Costco, Vons or Wal-Mart can easily be accomplished in twelve hours. Many shoppers combine the trip with a doctor visit or an evening in town to watch the latest movie in a theater. Slowly the Mexicans are finding out which items are desired, making the purchases themselves and putting them in their stores. Even though Costco and other big box stores have built outlets in Mexicali, most of the residents cross the border to shop. Many of the products found in Mexican stores are not items Yanks use. The stores cater more to the Mexican eating habits and many items desired by the U.S. citizen are available in the Costco and Wal-Mart store only a few miles to the north.

My daughter, Kusum, just left in a travel van with the antique furniture she is taking to her home in Oakland, CA. She is trying to make the drive to the bay area from Phoenix in a day. I keep forgetting that she is 33 and can do long drives. My ability to make such a marathon would not be something I would attempt at my age. I need a nap.

Furniture: A good tip regarding furniture for anyone wanting to move to Mexico is this: Items you have in the states may not be suitable for life in Baja or wherever you go. The hassle of moving a huge truckload of household items can be expensive. If you have children who need furniture, as many do when first leaving home, it may be a good time to pass these fixtures on. Even a garage or furniture sale would be advisable because the money you get for the goods sold minus the cost of shipping items down to Mexico would be more than enough to purchase items for replacement made in Mexico. In other words travel light when moving and replace what you can wherever you move.

Also people in Baja developments sell their furniture if health reasons develop and they decide to return to the states. Prices are usually reasonable because they want to sell things quickly and they are not concerned with making a profit on their garage sales. Children of parents who inherit a home in Mexico with all the furniture have no desire to keep the belongings of their parents. They also sell off the items at a 'get rid of' price. Word of mouth or sale notices on bulletin boards usually announce such liquidations.

Chapter 13
Ask a Lot of Questions

The best way to find out anything about how to move to Mexico and what to do, besides buying this book, is to ask those who reside where you are moving. Usually there is one person who is a wealth of information and he or she is usually willing to help in any way to make the move more enjoyable. The person we found we have known for six years. Here is his story.

Ed moved to El Dorado Ranch thirteen years ago when the development was just getting started under the new ownership of Pat Butler. He claims he is a type A person, which is considered goal-oriented and needing to get things done right away. He was moving to a country and a culture whose theme song is "Manana." In other words, 'getting it done yesterday' meets a culture, 'if you can not get it done today there is always tomorrow.' Guess who won that battle? Ed says it took three years before he gave up the fight.

Today he is content with his life in El Dorado. He runs his house just like he did back in the States. He has all the conveniences he would have in the States except his cost of living is reduced. Ed also says he only goes up to the States for medical visits and does any needed shopping at that time.

The swimming pool was in place in 2005 when we visited.

Thirteen years ago the development was made up of only a few houses and a large solar community in one area of the site. The National Pen Company owed the land before the present developer, Pat Butler, bought it. When Pat purchased the property, he wanted to give the investors in the development something to come and enjoy. Tennis courts and a golf course were the first things made available to the land purchasers and those who lived in the solar section of the ranch.

Ed purchased several plots, built his house and put rental homes on the other sites. People needed places to stay on the Ranch and the rental business was booming. He also gave people tours who were interested in buying into the development. According to Ed he did very well in the sale of land to future residents.

When Suzanne and I purchased our property in 2005 we were able to stay in one of his rentals free. Dan, our agent, rented from Ed and allowed us to stay in the house he rented by the month.

Where the Ranch is located was a former farm or Ejido community. The area is quite large and only a small portion of the property is used for development. What attracted me to the site was the location of the Ranch away from the town of San Felipe. Being seven miles to the north gives the residents a sense of living in a community unto themselves.

If they need to shop for items not found in the neighboring stores, the journey to San Felipe is still short. Small strip malls have developed on the main road near the Ranch which allows the residents to purchase gas, medication, pizza, wine, vegetables, coffee, American breakfasts, and Bud Light just to name a few. The last item mentioned should be stricken off the list because real beer drinkers know any Mexican beer is much better than the cheap U.S. mass-produced beers, watered down with no flavor.

The next attraction the Ranch held for me was the view of the Sea of Cortez and the mountain range behind the development. The properties on the hillside are staggered. The home sites behind the ones in front are located between the two lots in front of them. This way the homes are not blocked from the ocean views by a neighbor's home in front. Also, height limits are 15 feet. This restriction helps maintain the ocean views for everyone. Ranch-style homes also have stairways leading up to their rooftops. One portion of the roof is usually tiled, and some are set up with stoves for outdoor barbeque entertainment and patio furniture for enjoying the sunset and views. A few might also have small refrigerators for keeping the good Mexican beer cold. Sorry Bud Light, you are not allowed.

The golf course is another attraction of the Ranch

The sun rises out of the Sea of Cortez in the morning. When the clouds over the mainland of Mexico are present during the rainy season, sunrises can be spectacular. The same heavenly show is possible during sunsets over the mountain range separating San Felipe and the Ranch from the Pacific Ocean. Because the location of the 10,000 ft.-high mountains, all the pacific moisture is cut off from the Sea of Cortez and a desert climate exists. The only amount of rain reaching this Sonora Desert area comes from the occasional hurricanes sweeping the bottom portion of Baja or a freak thunderstorm. An occasional winter downpour may also get past the mountain range to the west of the Ranch. Two or three inches of rain is the yearly amount of precipitation. The locals make jokes about the lack rainfall all the time: "We got six-inches of rain in that last storm."

When I question the local as to how this is even possible, his response is: "Six inches between rain drops."

Some real funny people live down here.

Chapter 14
The Move is Upon Us

When the time to move to Mexico approached it came towards us like a runaway train heading down the tracks without brakes. No sidetracks existed in order to slow the moving date down. Friends made commitments to help with the move and I was dependent upon their schedules and not mine.

My best friend Scott offered to bring his huge trailer he uses to move his hobby around. He is a tractor guy and owns three of them at last count with a smaller one stashed somewhere where his wife, Pam, cannot see it. She understands his love for tractors but does not share to the same extent his passion for this farming machine. Seeing many types of farm vehicles at tractor shows, pulling heavy weights in the tractor pulls, or plowing the fields next to where the events are held each year is not her idea of a perfect weekend. You either love these farm implements or not.

I have gone to many tractor shows with Scott and have enjoyed the fair-like atmosphere. The smell of Kernel Corn roasting in the big cookers, fried chicken and turkey legs served to the sightseers and washed down with a Bud Light. Good taste in beer is not available.

Visas: Scott was available to bring a load of furniture to Mexico around the weekend of May 20. This date was almost a whole month before the time period when we thought about moving. The lease for our apartment lasted until the end of June and my last day of substitute teaching would be the week of May 27.

It was now the end of March. Suzanne and I went down to El Dorado Ranch for one more visit and to look for places to rent. We went through the paces of getting our tourist visas, which would last for six months, knowing we would have to renew them in September. Ed Jones told us that the tourist visa would be good for a while and not to rush into getting the higher-level visas like the FM-2 or FM-3. Since we were renting and owned only a lot the FM-1 or tourist visa would be fine. Until you are sure that the life style in Mexico is what you want and you can handle not having Starbucks, Olive Garden and Best Buy just down the road, then stay with the basic visa until you do.

This is a wise step for anyone thinking about becoming an expatriate in any foreign country who has never lived in another culture before. I lived in Europe for about three years total and abroad from the States for more than 10 years including longer stays in Australia, India and many adjacent countries. Suzanne, on the other hand, had never lived in a foreign country before. I would occasionally hear her describing the move to her friends as though we were moving to Outer Mongolia. The only food items served would be yak steaks and goat curd, and the meals would be washed down with some type of rice beer made by the women of the village with their bare feet during the festival of Mung. There is no festival of Mung, but I am sure moving to a foreign country can feel like the previous description for someone making such a transition for the first time.

In reality, we were moving to a gated community called El Dorado Ranch, which is only 100 miles south of the border from California. San Felipe, the nearby town, is quickly changing from a quiet fishing village into a destination for weekend vacationers, full time residents and desert-racing enthusiasts wanting to observe the Baja 250, 300, 500 and 1000. The events come right through the outskirts of town and the excitement created is unavoidable. Those who moved to the area for the peace and quiet can still have that by simply staying at home during the events and avoid going into San Felipe for a few days.

By April the antiques were gone. Suzanne's brother Michael drove out from Ramona, California with a large U-Haul truck filled with many of his possessions. He planned to make the house in New River livable while he slowly did the remodeling work. Michael was able to empty half the truck and drive to our place. He loaded the items including Suzanne's mother's furniture. We were now down to the bare essentials, which included our bed, just purchased the year before, the new couch in the living room, and several lamps, tables and chairs. We planned on purchasing dressers and other furniture items in Mexico that best fit the Mexican style of living.

Moving: This is a tip for those about to move. If you are not attached to any furniture and think it will look better in your children's homes, give it to them. It will be much easier to purchase in Mexico what you need instead of having to haul something that you may end up selling anyway. The knotty pine furniture I have seen in Mexico looks good in the Mexican style homes built on the Ranch and in other developments south of San Felipe. It is much easier to buy items there instead of paying the cost of hauling furniture from the States.

Chapter 15
Here We Go

For two weeks Suzanne spent days packing the items we would use in Mexico and setting aside the things we only stored between moves and never used. The second group went to Goodwill at a drop-off station only two miles from our house. Since our move down from Flagstaff to Peoria, AZ we have given many carloads of items to this institution. The feeling of 'letting stuff go' was like removing a backpack of rocks from your shoulders. The rocks may look good in storage, but if we never use them, why were we carrying them around with us wherever we went? If you have not used something in a year there is a good chance you do not need it. By the time we were all boxed-up and ready for Mexico, we probably had given away two-thirds of our household items no longer used or needed.

The stage was set. I was scheduled to work until May 18 in the Paradise Valley School District as a substitute teacher. I retired from teaching in 2008 but still kept my foot in the door of education while Suzanne worked and finally retired in 2010. I had put one last year into teaching in the Phoenix area and now I was done.

Scott brought his huge tractor-trailer to our apartment in the early morning of the 18th and headed off to the airport for a quick school-related trip to Albuquerque, New Mexico for two days. I finished work, came home for a quick nap and headed off to New River with Suzanne to meet her brother. We picked up his small trailer, which I was borrowing and took him out to dinner for his birthday. We celebrated Michael's birthday and returned home. I parked the smaller trailer in front of the large trailer. I went to bed not knowing who would be helping me load the items going down to Mexico on Friday.

Several weeks before, I had paid for a trailer hitch to be put onto my Blazer so I could pull Michael's trailer. I used the U-Haul rental company to obtain a trailer hitch because they quoted me the best price. The Blazer was becoming a real Baja vehicle. and it now could pull a load as well as carry lots of boxes in the back. I was ready for the move, and the day was finally here.

The weekend before the move I discovered a work force of men outside of the Home Depot on Thunderbird off the 101 in Peoria. I asked them if anyone would be available for work next week and I was assured there would be workers to help with any loading of trailers. I went into Home Depot to purchase tarps needed to cover the trailers and stock up on ropes to tie down any and all items subject to the gale-force winds on the 300-plus mile trip to our new Baja home.

While in the store I mentioned to a clerk I planned to use some of the workers waiting outside. I received a reaction, which reminded me I was in Arizona, the state with the harshest laws aimed at the Mexican population and any Hispanic person seeking work. The Governor of Arizona won her election based on signing a bill, which allowed the local sheriff permission to stop anyone who might look like a foreigner. In other words any Hispanic looking individual was up for grabs. Hispanics needed to carry documents showing that their presence in the States was legal or face deportation. The worker in the store held the view of many residents in the Phoenix area. Anyone of color, especially brown, needed to be checked for proper documentation. My hiring these men to work just encouraged them to live here.

I returned on Thursday morning and found two men who needed work. I promised them two or three hours of labor. As they got into the car two other men came out of the coffee shop at McDonalds and began knocking on my window as I was driving away. I guess they felt they were the next workers in line, but they were not on the street at the moment I needed them. One of the men in my car spoke excellent English and said he was born in Texas. He did most of the translation for the other worker whose origins were unknown to me.

After arriving at the apartment ten minutes after I picked up my workers, the men set to work getting all the big items out of the apartment. My plan was to load the big trailer first and fill in the spaces in between with boxes and loose items. Next we would load the smaller trailer with mostly boxes and lighter items. Having never pulled a trailer with my six-cylinder Blazer before, I wanted to be sure that I did not overload the engine. Scott owned a large Ford truck and hauled tractors all the time, so I was assured the load he pulled would not be too much for his vehicle.

As the workers started to move the heavy items onto the trailers, the one from Texas started up a conversation with his partner and me. I knew enough Spanish vocabulary to know what they were talking about when they spoke to each other but none of the details. When he asked me where we were moving, he seemed shocked when I told him Mexico. I do not think he spent much time across the border and the thought of gringos going one way while Mexicans attempted to go the other way baffled him. I tried to explain to him that many people from the northern states and Canada moved to communities within Mexico and had been doing so for years. He shook his head in a manner indicating disbelief. At the same time he understood how retired people who want a similar life style as they had when working might choose to live in a country where the dollar bought more. This list included housing, food, and services.

His partner still had family in Mexico and understood what I was saying. He was a Mexican and knew the benefits and lifestyle of his home country. He may have had a Green card in order to work in the states but I never asked him. I figured by the time this book is on the market, Sherriff Joe could not get me. My hiring a possibly illegal worker in Arizona is not a worry, and I do not make decisions based on the belief system as many of the conservative citizens in this state do.

"Giving work to someone with brown skin encourages them and they keep coming to the States."

Another comment: "They are taking away all our jobs."

I have heard these arguments many times and have not found them to be true. What I have observed regarding the types of work the Hispanic population does in Arizona is that those jobs are not being taken away from non-working citizens. The work in this State includes yard maintenance, and road construction in 110-degree weather. The hotel and restaurant industries providing the services to keep these businesses going also are on the list. I feel I could devote a couple of chapters to this subject or even write a separate book about it. Instead I need to catch up with my move and all the fun associated with such a transition.

Both workers loaded the two trailers. The Green card worker knew how to tie down the loads using the rope and tarps I had purchased at the Home Depot the week before. I returned the men to their starting place near Home Depot and the 101 and paid them well. I returned to the almost empty apartment which contained a couple of sleeping mats, TV and kitchen items, enabling Suzanne and myself to eat and camp out while making the transition. Scott was returning in the evening and had scheduled a final sporting event in Phoenix. The Diamondbacks were playing Colorado and baseball was a sport both Mexico and the U.S. shared. I slept in the apartment for a few hours before Scott arrived.

Late in the afternoon, Scott arrived from New Mexico after his meeting regarding his work at Northern Arizona University in Flagstaff. Rested enough to enjoy the game, have a beer and eat baseball junk food, we returned to the empty apartment to sleep and ready ourselves for the trip ahead. The idea of taking small loads of household items across the border came from others who had accomplished the feat before.

Ed Jones originally came from the States and used a similar approach. He moved his household items to a storage shed near the border where he crossed. He probably rented a U-Haul or some other company to get the items to the border. None of the American hauling companies allow their trucks or trailers to go into Mexico. When I was trying to rent a trailer to do just that, the U-Haul people said, "Once you cross the border you have purchased the trailer. "

The charge would be put on the credit card the company had on file when the trailer was rented in the first place, and the cost would be higher than the value of the trailer in order to thwart such attempts at hi-jacking U-Haul trailers to Mexico. If I were moving to Canada there would be no problem. U-Haul has locations in Canada. The Canada is not a third-world country, and the relationship with our northern neighbor is much different than with our southern neighbor. They are white, speak English or French and were founded by England just like the U.S.

If a Mexican company set themselves up allowing trailers and trucks to cross into the States and return with items, it would become a prosperous company in a short amount of time. They could charge a reasonable rate on their equipment and place a tracking device on the items rented.

I was lucky enough to have a brother-in-law who owns three trailers, and one of them turned out to be the perfect size for me to use. I could have rented a trailer from a Mexican company on the Ranch, who moved people down to San Felipe.

The problem was that their rates were high. I could purchase a trailer, do the job and have $1000 left in my pocket for the same amount of money he would charge. I suppose there are residents who live in the San Felipe area who have the money to be moved by this man and his large truck. There are those like myself who can still manage such a move on our own.

During this transition time Suzanne committed to several house sitting-jobs for friends going on trips. She left the same night for one of those jobs the day Scott returned from New Mexico. After we left with the first load of household goods for Mexico, she and I were officially gypsies and would not sleep in our own bed again until she completed all her obligations in the States and came with me on our last hauling trip a month later. It was now May 20 and Suzanne would be coming down to Baja on June 19.

Around 9 a.m. we were ready to leave after hooking up both the trailers and pointing them in the direction of Mexico. I had a neighbor couple, each with a different view of Mexico. Joe had been to Mexico and loved to fish. He enjoyed the pace of life along with the food and drink of our southern neighbor. His wife held a different vision. She could not understand how anyone from the States could move to Mexico, let alone live there. She said she would pray for us to be safe and have nothing bad happen during our transition. She was sure all of Mexico was a war zone and nobody with any sense would ever even think of going there. She was sure this was going to be the last time she would lay eyes on Suzanne and me and that we would soon be in the headlines of the local paper: "The Couple Who Disappeared in Baja"

We are packed and ready to pull out of Peoria, AZ

On the Road Again became my theme song, playing over and over again in my mind as I headed south on the 101, west on the 10 and southwest on the 85 connecting us to the 8. From Gila Bend, highway 8 pointed west towards Yuma and the border into the land of 'no return'. The 'no return' part is the belief many Americans hold based on news stories. One TV station in particular, named after an animal found in the forests of America with a big bushy tail, has been using fear tactics for years in order to paint a picture of a scary world. The people who follow the news on this station may have a difficult time getting a balanced news report. They will probably remain in their homes and communities afraid of the world surrounding them with different cultural values and speaking foreign languages. Their mantra: "Ignorance is Bliss".

Dateland: For anyone who travels west on highway 8 towards Yuma, there is a 'must stop' along the way. I have mentioned Dateland before but now you will get the detailed report. When I first started traveling to Mexico from Flagstaff to San Felipe six years before, Dateland became the halfway-point marker in miles. Scott and I made it a ritual stop in order to drink one of their date shakes. The dates are blended with vanilla ice cream and purchased to enjoy while driving along the road either to Mexico or returning to Flagstaff.

Six years ago this little oasis consisting of a date palm orchard, sandwich and shake stand, plus a gas station. It stood all by itself next to a memorial marker for WWII pilots from a certain squadron in the war. The old highway 80 was the road passing right next to this location but highway 8 has now replaced the old route. A driver has to take the exit to Dateland in order to taste the shake delight.

Two major things happened to this little rest stop over the years, which changed the experience of having a date shake forever. The first one happened in 2008 or 2009. The little sandwich and shake stand went through a major remodeling. A large company either bought the location or the owner got a loan and put in a Quizno's sandwich restaurant. The gift shop was enlarged and new restrooms put in to accommodate the large crowds stopping there. New blenders were purchased, operating faster and more efficiently. They grind up the dates into smaller pieces thus allowing the shake to be consumed with ease. A new and modern Texaco gas station was also built, and this led to the demise of the older Chevron station across the road.

The remodel of the little shake stand has brought a tremendous increase in business to the once tiny oasis. With the change I am now part of the legion of old cronies who visited this rest stop before the additions and can say things like, "I remember when Dateland was just a hole in the wall and the date shakes were difficult to drink. Things were much harder back then. You really had to work for what you got."

This last statement is the one change I miss. With the new blenders, the dates are totally mixed into the drink and only small pieces of dates can be found. All the date bits flow smoothly through the straw and the shake is easily sucked up and digested. I missed the old shakes containing date pieces too large to drink. These larger pieces would clog the straw and the only way one could continue to drink the shake was to blow into the straw, thus dislodging the large date piece out the other end.

The skilled drinker of the shake would then have to move the straw to another part of the shake cup and continue drinking until another large piece of date found its way to the sucking end of the straw and again blocked the flow of the shake into the drinker's mouth. This ritual would continue until the shake was drained and only 10 or 15 large pieces of dates remained at the bottom of the cup.

This old method of date-shake drinking took time and energy but this is the positive aspect of the ritual. The drinker would be totally entertained while driving on a part of the highway with little in the way of scenery and sights of interest. By the time the routine of drinking one of these old fashion shakes was completed, the driver would be very close to either Gila Bend, if he was driving east, or Yuma if he was driving west.

Of course, any storyteller of past events in history has to spice up the adventure with exaggerations and comments about how things used to be. I believe Mark Twain was the master of this skill. I am still amazed how he could turn a simple tale of a boy, with the job of whitewashing a fence, into a detailed description of wit and deceit. Tom Sawyer was able to persuade a troop of boys into paying him with artifacts and pocket riches so they too could have the privilege of painting a fence with whitewash and be the better for doing so. The story is genius, pure genius.

After Dateland appeared in our rear-view mirror, Yuma was the next city on highway 8 and only an hour away. The single hill on the whole trip was the pass through a desert mountain range called Dome Valley. These desert chains were not high and little plant growth appeared on the sides and tops of these hills. Their beauty appeared in the sharp ruggedness of the shape and dimension each hill presented. Most of these desert mountain chains are the result of geological uplift and are sculptured by winds. Breezes are a constant in the desert. Along with occasional rains coming either in the weather patterns of summer thunderstorms or the winter rains from the Pacific, the desert hills, molded by nature, are a beauty to behold.

Instead of going through Yuma and taking the 95 to the border of San Luis we took the 195 off highway 8. This is an alternative route recently built so that residents, trucks and other vehicles heading to Mexico or the American side of San Luis do not have to travel through Yuma and add to the traffic congestion. The alternative route has little traffic and we soon found ourselves in the outskirts of San Luis on the U.S. side. There is a town of San Luis on the Mexican side as well and this was our destination.

Chapter 16
The Border and Everything It Stands For

The Mexican border dividing the small community of San Luis about 35 miles southwest of Yuma is a small crossing. Because San Luis was a small border crossing I was hoping a couple of gringos pulling a couple of trailers would not be noticed. As cars approach the Mexican side there are two lanes for the vehicles to go through. One is for those who have nothing to declare and the other for those who need to declare goods so the Mexican government can tax the items. I decided to try the "nothing to declare" lane. All the items were household articles, and only the couch and a few other items were less than a year old. I really did not know what to expect because Ed Jones had not filled me in on any details as to what might happen. He made the move thirteen years ago. The rules then did not apply to what I would be facing at the present moment.

As we entered Mexico, a woman guard stepped out in front of the car and simply directed Scott and me to pull over to the left and park in the area where cars go when they have something to declare. Scott was my translator. When the questions started flying, I stepped back and let Scott do his best to get the answers we needed in order to move on. The first number coming from the mouth of the border guard was $900. Scott had been studying Spanish for years but to this day he still could not figure out what this number referred to. His wife, Pam, spoke fluent Spanish but she was not with us. We were on our own as far as making any headway as to any taxes we may be charged. The guards instructed us to untie the blue tarps covering the furniture so they could peek in and get an idea as to what we were bringing into Mexico.

A period of time passed with the guards talking between themselves after inspecting the trailer contents. Finally a number of $75 was presented to us. Scott thought the woman was asking for $75 for each trailer. After the number of $900 had been thrown around for a few minutes, $75 for each trailer sounded much more reasonable. The border guard took me over to a small office where other people, mostly Mexicans, were paying duty on items they had purchased in the States.

A nicely dressed young Mexican lady was just putting a designer handbag back into a box with the name of some store like Macys or I. Magnum on the side. She handed the officer behind the counter 100 pesos or around $9 for the duty. Any new furniture brought across the border might cost the person hundreds of dollars. It might be wiser to travel to Mexicali on the border, purchase the same item for less, pay no duty and bring it down to your house in Mexico. When one purchases anything in Mexico there is no tax to pay.

Finally the woman guard approached the agent in the office and gave him a number. That figure was 325. I did not know if she meant pesos or dollars. I should have realized she was using the currency of her country, pesos. This was the total amount for both trailers and cars both filled to the brim with boxes and household items. 325 pesos equaled $28.

During the time we crossed the border and paid the tax on goods being brought into Mexico the numbers, starting at 900 dollars, dropped to $75 per trailer and finally $28 for everything. Do you think I argued about having to pay this last amount or even attempted to put up any resistance as to how they figured out the amount I needed to pay. No way. I was ecstatic. I paid the officer.

Scott and I headed to the closest gas station and money exchange counter. The money conversion office was located at the Pemex station situated near the entrance to the toll road heading towards Mexicali. We filled up, bought our pesos and grabbed a few snacks for the trip down south.

The toll road is a highway built from Mexicali through the heart of Mexico. The Mexican government has been working on this expressway for years and the section I paid to use from San Luis over to highway 5 is now completed. As I traveled to the Ranch over the years I would come down during Christmas and sometimes during the spring. In the last four years I have started to use the San Luis border crossing because I heard about the highway. I wanted to avoid going through the busy city of Mexicali.

I now know a shortcut through Mexicali, which takes me directly to highway 5. The route goes through the wealthier suburbs of the capital where large homes are surrounded by walled separations and guarded gates. A Toyota dealership and large shopping complexes line the sidewalks through this back road. Other than the few taco and ice cream carts rolling up and down the street, one would think they were in any section of a community in the States. The road does pass through the middle and lower-class section of the city. The differences are staggering, especially for new visitors to Mexico who witness the separation of the classes for the first time.

Two minutes on the toll road took us to our next stop. In the States where there are agricultural stops or checks stations to see if any fruits, vegetables, or illegal residents are brought into a state or the U.S., Mexico has their military checks. They are looking for the possibility of any weapons headed into their country. As we approached the checkpoint I knew what to do by now. I exited the car and untied the tarp covering the household items in the trailer. This allowed the guard with the MK 37, or whatever type of automatic weapon he carried, to look into the trailer. Seeing I was bringing household items into Mexico with the intent on living here seemed to be a topic of amusement among his military friends. The conversation was too fast for me to understand everything said, but maybe the idea behind the discussion went something like this:

"Hey amigo, why are these gringos moving down into Mexico when so many Mexicans are trying to get into the States to find work and live?"

"I do not know Juan, but I can tell you this. Many of them are older and seem to be at the age of retirement. Some are younger but I have seen the younger ones returning to the states after a short stay. They bring house items in their cars so the younger gringos must have a casa where they stay. Almost all of them seem to be heading towards towns that are near the Sea of Cortez or the Pacific Ocean. I saw the same thing when I worked on the Tijuana border last year. There are many gringos moving into Mexico and many Mexicans trying to move to the States. I have often thought, why don't they have a land swap? Mexico could give the coast in Baja to the Americans and the U.S. could give the middle of California back to Mexico?"

"Why the middle of California?"

"If you go to the middle of California that is where all the food is grown. That is also the area where many Mexican workers go to find work. I visited central California once and everyone in the fields was a Mexican. Not one gringo was out in the 100-degree sun picking the crops that go to the food stores in America."

"Ay Chihuahua. That is hard work. I think America would starve if there were no Mexican workers in the fields doing that type of work."

"You are right amigo. If there were no workers doing this difficult labor, no one would be able to grow food in America. The migrant labor force is needed throughout the States. This is why I think the idea of making a trade of land is good. Give all the coast of Baja to the gringos where they can build resorts and houses. Give the land in central California to the Mexicans so they can live there and not have to worry about crossing the border each year to find work in the fields that grow food."

"What a great idea, Raul. You should run for governor and present this idea to the Mexican and American governments."

"No way, Juan. I may have great ideas, but I am not wealthy enough to be a politician. I still have my career in the army in Mexico. I want to be a sergeant some day and have my own jeep to drive around and order my men to do the work we are doing right now."

"OK Raul, but I still think your ideas are good and would help with a lot of these problems between America and Mexico."

"Juan, are we done with this gringo? He only seems to be taking household items down to San Felipe. He looks crazy enough to survive in Mexico and I am sure the money he spends in the community will help the citizens of San Felipe when he buys food and other things."

"Yes Raul, we can let him go. We are done solving the problems between the U.S. and Mexico for one day."

The military stop was the last roadblock until we reached another such checkpoint about twenty miles north of El Dorado Ranch. The toll-road was like a highway in the states. We could drive at speeds of 65 to 70 miles an hour or 110 to 120 km per hour. The cost for a car to get onto the toll road was 12 pesos and with a trailer around 19 pesos. When we exited the toll road the cost for a car and trailer was 24 pesos. The peso fluctuates between 11 and 11.5 pesos to the dollar at the present time. The charge was not much for driving on an expressway vs. driving on the side roads clogged with traffic and slow moving cars or trucks.

Driving on side road to main highway 5

We arrived at the Ranch after driving on highway 5 for about three hours. Usually the trip takes two hours. Road crews are working on a large section of the road about 40 miles south of Mexicali. At the present time the Mexican government is spending a lot of money fixing the roads and making Mexico driver-friendly. The government sees the future of Baja and other parts of Mexico having a large population of Canadians and Americans retiring or vacationing in the coastal communities south of the border. The expression "Build it and they will come" from the movie *Field of Dreams*, could not be more appropriate in this instance.

Road construction on highway 5 towards San Felipe

By making the access into Mexico easier to drive, more Americans, trying to escape the cold winters of the northern states and high prices of living in the southern states or Arizona, would be able to drive safely to retirement communities in Mexico. The only Americans I know who have made the move to this country are the ones who visited Mexico in the past. They fell in love with the culture and the pace of life and do not believe the news stories produced by the TV stations in America.

There are problems along some border cities due to the "War on Drugs." There are also many killings every day in the inner cities of America, either gang-related or otherwise, and many times drugs are the reason. I do not visit the towns on the border with the problems nor do I take the inner city tour through the gang areas of America.

Americans with the "huevos" (balls), to visit Mexico and any of the many communities within its borders where other foreigners live can find out for themselves the truth about life south of the border. Those Americans too afraid to explore and find out about Mexico should stay home. If they did visit they would probably not enjoy themselves. They might look down upon the Mexican population and constantly compare what they have in the States with what they cannot get in Mexico.

Living in a foreign country is not for the faint of heart. The benefits for me far outweigh the distractions and inconveniences I may face. I love the adventure one discovers in daily life and finding out how things are done in foreign lands.

Chapter 17
We Made It

Scott and I arrived at the house where we would be for the next three nights. Over the past six years of visiting El Dorado Ranch and getting to know the people I met a couple, Ken and his lovely wife Jill. While renting a house across the street from them three years before, Ken saw me on the porch using my computer and picking up his Wi-Fi signal. He invited Suzanne and me into their house for a drink in the evening and to visit. Both of them were hospitable and told us they owned a small casita behind their main house where they lived while building their main house. We rented the casita for the next three years from them and found the neighborhood and living arrangements perfect for our needs. Scott and I were going to stay in the casita again while making our furniture run to our next home in Mexico.

Ken and his wife are examples of a couple, no longer working, living comfortably in retirement. They could have retired anywhere in the States but chose to move to the Ranch and build the house of their dreams for a lot less than the cost they would have paid in the States.

S.A.F.E.

Being a retired sheriff from central California, Ken was into security. On the Ranch he started a home protection group called S.A.F.E. or Safety Assured for Everyone. The group is made up of volunteers who check on homes of people on their list when they are away either on vacation or visiting family in the States. The Ranch has their own security team patrolling the many homes found all over the development. S.A.F.E. is a volunteer group of men and women and an added source of security for the residents. Many Snowbirds, living on the Ranch, put their names on the list of residents wanting their houses checked while they were gone for the summer.

We pulled up to Ken's house around 7 p.m. after having dinner at the Playa de Oro (Beach of Gold). Playa is one of the most popular restaurants for the gringo population either on the Ranch or in one of the many other developments north of San Felipe. The prices of the meals were in dollars but pesos are accepted as well. Drinks and food cost more than other Mexican restaurants in the area but the menu selection and atmosphere made the prices worth the extra expense.

All major sporting events could be seen while having a beer at the bar or dinner in the dining area. Scott and I enjoyed our first cold beer after making the journey and pulling two trailers filled with most of a household of furniture over 300 miles from the Phoenix area to El Dorado.

Ken was home when we pulled in. Jill was gone, so it was boys' night out at the Rhino home. Ken acquired the nickname Rhino based on his last name, Reinstadler. There was plenty of room to park the SUVs and trailers in the circular driveway outside the wall marking Ken's property. After unpacking the suitcases we would need in order to make our stay comfortable, Ken brought out a bottle of wine. We sat out in the covered palapa in the back yard, enjoying the cool breezes coming in off the Sea of Cortez while sharing our border-crossing experience.

Ken told the story of his move to El Dorado. Like a lot of other people who live further than 300 miles from their destination, the idea of making a number of small trailer loads of furniture seemed too overwhelming. Several small loads of furniture over a distance of 500 miles or more would make the journey an expensive endeavor.

Ken was able to get a large truck and load it with all his belonging. He made the journey for about $900. I do not know if this price included the gas but I know that Ken needed to rent a vehicle from a private company and not U-Haul or Penske because none of the big rental businesses allow any of their trailers or trucks to cross into Mexico. Mexico does not have any of these types of businesses.

Gator attacking dog is Ken's landscaping sense of humor

Moving: There are private movers who charge outrageous prices to move you, and if you have thousands of dollars to spend, then so be it. Unless you are really attached to your belongings, I would suggest that you sell all large items of furniture that can be replaced.

Pack only clothes and articles, which are personal and take the thousands of dollars you would have spent on such a move and buy new furniture and household items when you reach your destination. I am told some of the best furniture comes from the mainland of Mexico, and with the money you would save from such a purchase you could get a new washer and dryer as well. These items, made by the big companies such as Hotpoint or Kenmore, are also sold in Mexico. The only difference I have noticed is that all the settings are in Spanish and you only have to translate and learn the words in order to wash and dry your clothes.

After an hour of wine and sharing information with Ken, Scott and I headed to the casita for some needed rest. We were to meet the agent renting the house for the owner at Roadrunner café for breakfast. The café is owned and run by an American and his Portuguese wife who purchased it from the original owner. They are making a go of it in the Baja sun.

The breakfast menu includes most of the basic items found in the States such as pancakes, eggs and omelets cooked the way you like them. I believe espresso and other coffee drinks are available. Payment in either dollars or pesos is accepted in this oasis of Americano food.

Summer hours were starting and the restaurant was only open until 11 a.m. due to the smaller population of residents living on the Ranch and in nearby developments during the warm summer months.

(**2014 update**. Roadrunner is now located at Playa de Oro across from the Saltito gate entrance to the El Dorado Ranch. A restaurant named The Diner is in the old Roadrunner location.)

After a filling breakfast and time spent waiting for the agent to arrive with a couple of workers, a phone call was made to re-establish the meeting place. The agent now told us to meet him at the house with a promise he and other man would arrive shortly to help unload the heavy items. We drove the few miles to the house, my new home south of the border. After twenty minutes all the characters helping with the move arrived.

In a little more than an hour the trailers were unloaded and contents piled into the house or garage. The agent gave me the key to make copies for myself. The first part of the move to Mexico was complete. The man who helped with the move was a Mexican-American, raised in Marin county near San Francisco and now working and living in the San Felipe area. I paid him well for the unloading help. I knew could count on him to do it again. Twenty-five dollars for a little more than an hour of work to complete the job insured he would be there. The price was worth it, and I felt relieved when the job was finished.

In Mexico and the States, food or drink is used to celebrate a job well done. Scott and I headed downtown after dropping off the trailers at Ken's house. We unhooked my trailer so that a parking space could be found with relative ease. A beer or two was a deserved reward for 'Mission Accomplished', or at least the first step in the process. Sitting in the Taco Factory with the cool breezes coming off the Sea of Cortez, which lay across the street from where we were on the Malecon, I knew the choice I made to do such a move was working out perfectly.

Scott, on the left, and me celebrating a job well done

Scott was amazed the trip had been completed without any real trouble. I told Scott I used a technique I learned when traveling throughout the world from 1970 to 1979. I have practiced the technique ever since my return to the States back in 1979. It is called visualization. The person using this technique keeps repeating the process of what they want to see happen over and over again in their head. They see the outcome being completed and actually visualize themselves in the act of completing it. I saw the border crossing being accomplished and driving down to the Ranch without complications or distractions. I also saw the trailers being unloaded with little trouble and a safe return for both of us. So far the technique was working out just fine.

Chapter 18
Second Load to Mexico

For the next two days, Scott and I basically relaxed, caught up on computer e-mail and wrote about the move on Facebook. A few of my friends were interested in Mexico and the relocation process, while a few probably thought we were crazy and would never be seen again. On Monday morning we were ready to return to the States. We packed, ate some breakfast and were on the road by 9 a.m. We returned through the Mexicali border using the newer east-side crossing. It is usually faster than the main gate located across from the town of Calexico on the California side.

At the crossing I was flagged by the border patrol to be searched at a separate area under a metal tent. The guard said I was still in the computer system because of last time I visited in March. At that time Suzanne and I declared some illegal vegetables and fruits, which needed to be tossed away. The guard said he would remove my name from the system so I would not be pulled over each time I entered the States. I thanked him and we drove off toward Yuma.

We both paid homage to the shakes in Dateland, drinking our ritualistic beverage in honor of the date trees found behind the oasis. Two hours later we were back in Phoenix. Scott drove off to run some errands and I crashed for an hour before planning on the next load I would be taking down within a week. Scott returned and stayed the night, driving to Flagstaff the next morning.

Tuesday and Wednesday were spent filling the small trailer and my Blazer with another load of household items from the apartment. I wanted to get as many of the large, bulky pieces of furniture into the hauler because this would be the last load I would be making with my brother-in-law's box on wheels. He needed the trailer for carrying his tools around when on jobs in California as well as helping with his move to New River just outside of Phoenix.

I mentioned earlier Michael had just purchased a bank-owned home and planned to fix it up, live in it for a few years and sell it when the housing market recovered. This same house would also be our address in the States and Suzanne and I could live in it at any time we needed to. We were really becoming gypsies with multiple addresses where we could live.

By Thursday the trailer was packed, as well as the car. Visibility of anything behind me now became limited to the side-view mirrors. Nothing could be seen using the rear-view mirror in the car other than boxes and household items touching the ceiling of the Blazer. My goal was to drive down to the Ranch, unload, and return by Saturday. The Memorial Day weekend was starting on Saturday and the number of people crossing over into Mexico would be high. For many visitors going to Mexico, the Memorial weekend was the end of the Mexico season. Soon hotter temperatures along with the winds from the south, bringing the humid weather, would be the norm.

After waking on Thursday morning I headed off to my last medical appointment in Phoenix. My heart doctor, Dr. Patel from India, said I needed a stress test to see how the generic medications I had switched to were working and how my heart was holding up. My appointment had been made several weeks earlier so off I went to the clinic without food or drink in my system. I had done these treadmill exercises before in Flagstaff, where the test was done on a gym-type walking machine with wires connecting all over my body and readings taken every few minutes. In Phoenix the procedure was much more involved.

The first thing I had to do never made it on the Flagstaff list of how to run a stress test. I was hooked up to an I.V. and injected with some radiation liquid intended to flow through my blood system. Next a picture of my upper torso was taken to see the condition of my blood flow in a rested state and to check for any blockages. With the I.V. still in my arm I was moved to the treadmill where I was hooked up just like in the Flagstaff office and monitored on the same type of machine measuring my heart rate. At my peak HBPM or heartbeats per minutes I was again injected with more radiation and continued on the hamster wheel for another minute before being reduced to a normal walk. The treadmill finally slowed down and stopped. One more stop at the photo machine to see if any blockages were occurring and I was finally free to go.

The procedure took about two hours and the time was now around ten o'clock. I was full of radiation, hungry and ready to get on the road again with my last trailer load of furniture. Breakfast became my first obligation. After one last visit to the 'Egg and I' just down the road from our apartment, I returned to the trailer. I hooked it up to the Blazer and tied down the load with my blue Home Depot plastic tarp made in China using the techniques learned by observing the helper who had wrapped the first load.

I called Suzanne, who was up in Flagstaff, and told her my change of plans. Since the time was now noon, the drive all the way to the Ranch was out of the question. Arriving at 7 or 8 at night was too late, and trying to push myself to finish the move would not be of any value to my health.

Pacing myself was important at this time. I decided to drive to Yuma, only three hours by car without a trailer or four hours with a trailer. Another stop for the ritual drink of a date shake and finally into Yuma by 4 o'clock to take advantage of the $39 special at Motel 6. A shower, quick nap and up in time to make it to Denny's for the early-bird special or in my case a veggie-burger and drink. Up by 6 and another early-bird special for breakfast at Denny's and I was on the road to the San Luis border crossing again for another adventure.

Upon arriving at the border I first exchanged some dollars on the U.S. side and then proceeded to the line to declare items being brought into Mexico. The last time I crossed with Scott we went through the 'Nothing to Declare' line and had to pay a minimal amount of money. I thought I should let the guards see my household items and not attempt to get through without paying a tax. I also hoped the fee would be less with only one trailer and a car full of goods.

The woman customs guard, who took care of us just days before, was not working at the time. Another male guard approached me and asked to look into the car and trailer. He spoke no English and his manner told me he was going to be a little more challenging than the woman who checked us on the last crossing. The guard motioned for a young man to come over and I soon found out he was to be the interpreter in the verbal haggling we would engage in as to how much the tax or fee would be.

The first number thrown at me was just like before. $900. This number seemed to the initial amount thrown at Americans bringing items down to Mexico, no matter how much they were bringing. Maybe a few Americans had paid this amount before and it seemed like a good amount to try and get again.

My translator spoke English with an American accent. I got a closer look at him and realized the man making the communication possible for me was either an ex-gangbanger from the states or an active one in hiding and living on the Mexican side in the town of San Luis. He seemed to be working for tips by helping the guards talk to the gringos who did not know enough Spanish to complete the needed discussions.

He wore his hair short and was covered in tattoos on his arms and upper body. I think the blue and red markings on his neck stating "Kill the Pigs" was a good indication he had lived a life of a gang member with no love for authority. My intuition told me he was not a butcher and the remark "Kill the Pigs" had nothing to do with his occupation or desire for people to eat the other white meat. He did a good job translating, while also telling me the guard I was dealing with was an asshole and really uptight. Wow, I was having a temporary relationship with a gangbanger and could add this fact to my 'things to do before I die' list.

I explained to my new English and Spanish speaking friend that I had crossed the border the previous Friday with two trailer-loads of household goods and was charged only 325 pesos or $28 in fees. After the border guard heard the translation he seemed to get mad and told my new ally from the States this was not possible. Producing the receipt from the previous trip to show the guard I was telling the truth seemed to agitate him even more. The $75 dollar amount paid in the previous crossing was also mentioned. I was asked how much the load was worth and I said it was difficult to put a dollar price on used items and clothing. At first I said $1000 but finally put the amount at $500. A few more exchanges and the Mexican guard finally arrived at 425 pesos for the tax. The charge was 100 pesos more than I paid for the two trailer-loads on the first trip but at the same time it was nowhere close to the first two amounts asked for when I crossed. I proceeded to the same office where money was collected on the previous Friday. I wanted to get the amount paid and be on my way.

All of a sudden another border guard came running over to us and he seemed excited about something. He was speaking quickly and loudly. My translator started asking me if I had brought some special type of medications with me. I told him I took heart medications but nothing unusual. After another burst of Spanish from the second guard to my tattooed friend, and another bit of information became known. The guard said something about radiation and a border machine picking up a high count on me as I walked over to the office to pay the tax on my belongings. I knew exactly what happened and explained to my ally: "I was given a stress test yesterday morning and the doctors put radiation into my bloodstream before I walked on a treadmill. I believe it takes two-and-a-half days for the radioactive material to be out of my body and today was only the first day."

After the guard was given the Spanish translation for my statement, he seemed to understand what had happened and waved good-by to me and walked away. I guess other gringos may have had this same test in the past and set off the meter measuring radiation materials coming across the border. I paid my fee, tipped my personal translator, and drove off to get gas. I was trying to arrive at the Ranch before noon.

Translator Fee: To this day I feel I did not tip my translator enough. He did a great job but I only had a few bucks on hand. For anyone else having a need for a person to help with the language, at least $10 should be paid for the job they perform. If I cross at San Luis again I will keep my eyes open for the person with 'Kill the Pigs' written on his neck. I've had time to think about the border experience and, without his help, I may have spent a lot of time explaining the value of my personal goods and my radioactive condition to the guards. I plan to give him more money because he deserved it. Tip well, my fellow travelers, and you will get good service, even if you don't eat pork.

Another quick stop at the military post on the toll road after filling with gas and I was on my way. The three-hour trip, while pulling a trailer, is usually shorter but the roadwork continued. I did not drive fast on the side roads built to divert the traffic around the highway to San Felipe.

Chapter 19
The Final Push

By noon I arrived at the casita where I stayed on my last trip. The owners, Ken and Jill, were on a trip, so they instructed me to leave the rent in a drawer and lock it up again when I left. Ken left me a dolly in the room so I could move the heavy file cabinets from the trailer into the new home.

Arrangements had been made to meet a Mexican worker at the gas station near the main gate of

Saltito Road around 2 p.m. After arriving a little early and waiting for almost half an hour I eventually decided the worker was a 'no-show'. I planned to head over to the house and keep an eye out for a possible worker walking along the road. An inner voice in the way of a feeling told me I could find a helper. Within two hundred yards of the Pemex station I spotted an older man, in his 50s, walking towards San Felipe.

"Quero usted trabajar?" I asked in my first-year school Spanish.

"Si" came the response and he started to run off a lot of Spanish my simple vocabulary would not handle. I asked him to speak 'mas despacio', and I soon discovered he was asking me to take him into town after the job was finished. I agreed and felt fortunate to have found someone willing to work for about an hour unloading my car and trailer.

We pulled up at the house. Armed with the few words I knew in Spanish, along with hand motions and pointing, we were able to communicate where each item went in the house and finish the job within an hour. My worker friend, Ramon, spoke no English and when he spoke quickly in Spanish, a simple 'mas despacio por favor' was all I needed to get him to repeat the sentence slowly, allowing me to pick up the few words I understood and make an educated guess as to what he was saying.

Today was Friday and it was Memorial weekend. On my drive down to the Ranch, almost every American making the journey from the states pulled a trailer with dune buggies or other types of four-wheeled-drive vehicles capable of going into rough terrain or up a sand dune with ease. I knew the town would be full of those who love the Baja and all the things you could do on a three-day weekend.

After unloading the vehicles we headed into San Felipe to return Ramon to his house in the barrio. He wanted me to see where he lived so that I could find him again when I needed someone to do a job. Ramon told me he had come to San Felipe from the southern part of Mexico five years before to help build the houses on the Ranch and in other developments springing up along the white sands of the Sea of Cortez. He worked as an electrician and knew how to wire a house and hook up other devices needing electrical energy.

When we reached his home, the difference between where he lived and the house my wife and I were moving into could not be compared.

A wire fence surrounded his home around six hundred to eight hundred square feet in size. A mixture of plaster and cardboard covered the walls. A palapa-type roof made of palm tree branches gave the house shade and protection from the weather and elements. When it came time to pay him, I pulled out a ten-dollar bill and a five-dollar bill. Handing him both bills was not difficult. The fact he was being overpaid did not seem to matter to me after dropping him at his house. Overpaying a worker for a small job in a third-world country at least gave me the satisfaction he would have food on the table that night and I would sleep the better for it.

I drove into town from Ramon's house still pulling the empty trailer behind me. My intent was to return to the oceanfront bar, The Taco Factory, to celebrate mission accomplished again with another beer. The town was undergoing a transformation due to the big Memorial Day weekend. The early arrivals were already here and the locals were setting up all their wonderful tourist items and off-road vehicles to rent so the gringos would be entertained and have something to do. No parking spots could accommodate a car with a trailer, so I decided to return to where I was staying. A quick shower and a short drive to

Playa de Oro for an early dinner and one of their margaritas became my focus.

Arriving at Playa de Oro with last load

On arrival at the restaurant near the Ranch, I noticed the parking lot filled with cars and trucks of every make and model. There was a band playing in the restaurant and standing room only seemed to be the norm. The American and Canadian population within a five-miles radius of the place had converged upon the bar, each one holding a drink in their hands. A poster on the wall told me it was a fund-raising party for the dog-neutering program in San Felipe, and the $5 cover charge helped pay for the band and the clinic to continue its services.

With no seat available inside the restaurant, I found a spot at one of the outdoor tables and ordered a margarita. It became my celebration drink for the moment. The outdoor tables were almost filled as well. I started to pay attention to the faces of these gringos, knowing many of them were going to be my neighbors and fellow expatriates in the area surrounding El Dorado Ranch.

The average age seemed to be around 60, with some of the older women possibly close to 80. I found out later, after living in the area, there happens to be a large number of single older women who have outlived their husbands and live alone in the different developments around San Felipe. The majority of the party population was singing along to the 60's and 70's music being played by the young Mexican band on stage. I even spotted an ex-rocker woman trying out her air guitar when a favorite song from her youth was played. I had my camera with me and decided to document some of the locals cutting loose and having fun. It reminded me of a seventh-grade sock hop with mostly women doing the dancing. Except now these teenage girls were living in an older body but the spirit of their youth lived on, not missing a beat. 'Rock On Baja Mama'

Old rockers dancing at Playa de Oro

I drank my first margarita and ordered a chicken dinner. I needed to eat and I knew I could not stay long because of my schedule of returning to Phoenix early the next morning. As I ate my meal, the next band set up and began to play. This older rocker, rumored to have started out in his youth playing with Santana, came from Tijuana. He was a 67 years old man with long black curly locks covering his head and hanging down to his shoulders. He continued to play the 60's and 70's music, which was the favorite of the present crowd. His guitar-playing ability was one of the best I had seen, and he would walk around the dinning room playing such great hits as 'G-L-O-R-I-A', 'I Heard it From the Grapevine' and one of the most popular songs in Baja, 'Margaritaville.'

Baja Mama playing air guitar behind real Rocker

The group of residents at the dance was the same age as those living in the retirement community in Peoria from which I was now moving, but they expressed one major difference from those in Arizona: 'Spirit.' It really did feel like the majority of those attending this fundraiser were young at heart and just happened to be operating in older bodies for the time being. They were really having a good time.

I finish my meal and ordered one last drink. I even made it to the dance floor when a few of my special songs were played. Because I was one of the few males daring to strut their stuff in front of the band, I was asked by another dancing Mama to 'cut the rug' with her. This was a fun bash and a great way to celebrate my move to Mexico. By 7:30 I knew I needed to leave. The party was going strong, but I realized I would not be getting up early if I remained. My return to the border as early as possible was necessary. I took a few pictures of the locals while eating dinner so I could post the party on Facebook and show the rest of the world how the retirees in Mexico were doing not *Wasting away in Margaritaville.*

I got to sleep by 9 and woke with the sunrise. Because this was a short trip I had very little to pack. 6:30 a.m. found me 'on the road again' and heading towards Mexicali and the border. A stop at the military check-post so they could see I was not carrying any weapons or other items illegal in Mexico and another stop at a tire store near the military check-point to get a quick cup of instant coffee to keep me sharp for the drive to the border.

Tire Information: One comment about the countless tire or llantera shops found everywhere in Baja. American tires are taxed at a steep rate when brought into Mexico. Mexico wants to sell their brand of tires. I suspect the Mexican tire is not as durable as the American tire and they wear out faster and fall apart. Most of the stores only sell used tires. There are at least ten tire stores found on the seven-mile drive to San Felipe from El Dorado.

Also, roadwork forces cars onto side dirt roads so extra stress is put on the rubber wheels of all vehicles. I am not sure how the numerous tire stores all stay in business, but I suspect the reason is that the Mexican tires have a short life cycle. In Baja you need good rubber for the many dirt roads you have to travel on and for the countless four-wheel-drive vehicles used to explore the back country in order to see the beauty of the Baja and its coastline.

Arriving at the border around 9:30 on Memorial Day weekend was a misjudgment on my part. The thought of Mexicans wanting to go to the States for the weekend in large numbers never occurred to me. My thinking process: many Americans would be coming down to Baja with all their toys for traveling along the beaches and back roads. This last statement is true, but the opposite was also true. Many Mexicans were going to the States to buy items they either resold in Mexico or for personal use. Costco, Wal-Mart and other big chain stores in El Centro and Calexico do a tremendous amount of business serving the east side of Baja, and I am sure the warehouse stores in San Diego do a good business serving the west coast strip of land down to Ensenada.

The line to the border looked to be more than an hour. I did not have a Sentri pass as yet, so I had to go with the flow and slowly creep along towards the crossing while watching the countless merchants walking through the lines of cars selling the newest videos, sun protectors, food items and washing your car. This last item I purchased almost every time I crossed the border. Men with window squeegees, a squirt bottle of water and a few rags patrolled the sea of dusty vehicles waiting in line. For pocket change they would clean off the layer of dust accumulated on the side roads coming up from San Felipe. For ten pesos or around 90 cents, I could get the whole car wiped down and windows washed. When finished, my car looked as good as if I had just driven through a $5 speedy-wash in the States.

Finally I made it to the front of one of the seven lines leading back into the States. A woman guard was at the station I came to and I started a conversation with her, while hoping my name was off the list of those who tried to bring illegal vegetables and fruit across the border. She told me my name was no longer on such a list but I still had to go to the second check out area because I was showing signs of radiation and it had to be checked out. Not only did she send me to the area of 'extreme search', she had to shut down her stall and walk me over to the station to make sure I arrived at the correct destination.

Radiation coming into the States seemed to be a serious offense needing to be checked out in great depth. The woman guard passed me off to the serious border patrol people in the same area where the search for illegal fruits and vegetables took place. A male guard began the intense questioning and scanning of my body and car. Both were done in different locations. I explained I received a stress test two days before and that the radiation took 2.5 days to pass from the bloodstream. The guard still had to do the thorough search.

Even with the explanation, the process took an hour. I was scanned twice and the Blazer with trailer also received a double dose of radiation inspection. The guards needed to be sure the readings on the detector were only coming from me and not from some hidden compartment in the car. Finally the 'all clear' sign was made and I was off again to regain my strength and quench my thirst with another date shake 75 miles away.

When I reached Yuma I returned to the Denny's just off the highway and wolfed down the senior breakfast. My first meal of the day at 10 a.m. was later than usual but well received. Now I was heading towards Dateland on the 8, but first I had the immigration stop and Dome Valley pass to negotiate. With these out of the way, the long and straight road to Mohawk Valley lay before me with nothing in the way of scenery or points of interest as a distraction.

Thirty miles out of Yuma I heard a bang, thump, thump and then nothing. My first thought was the trailer fell off but a quick check in the rear view mirror dispelled that fear. Pulling over to the side of the road allowed me to get out of the car and view a section of tire from the right side of the trailer now added to the other pieces of tire art laying alongside the highway, complimenting the desert landscape. The tire lost about a third of its tread but remained in the inflated stage of life so I could still drive, but slowly. A Chevron station sign told me I was near the possibility of getting help and I headed down the road at 20 mph.

I soon arrived at the new development on the south side of highway 8, built within the past 5 years for those wanting to retire in the desert and still be close to a city such as Yuma. The Chevron station turned out to be the modern version of service stations today. Gas and oil for the cars and a large snack section selling the top-brand junk-food items for the traveler on the road. No garage for repairs existed.

The woman inside the station told me about a tire store across highway 8 in the small town of Wellton. She also thought it closed at noon on Saturday. Since this was Memorial Day weekend she was sure the shop would be empty.

I looked at my watch. The time was now 12:45. Thanking her for the information, I took the overpass to the small agricultural community located off the old highway 80 and found the closed store called Ed Whitehead's tires. Just as she predicted, the store was closed and not a sole in sight. In fact, the whole town seemed empty. This probably meant the long weekend in a small community like Wellton gave the locals a reason to take off and enjoy a few days away from the hot, flat desert landscape. Going to San Diego for the beaches or the mountains for the pine trees and cooler temperatures would be good alternatives for the residents wanting a change. The new development on the other side of highway 8 seemed to be getting all the roadside business so any local restaurant or gas station remained closed.

What to do? The trailer could not make the trip to Dateland and I did not want to stay the weekend in Wellton watching weekend movie re-runs on HBO at a local hotel. I found someone in the Border Patrol office across the street from Ed's tires and got the phone number of the store. Someone answered, and after telling him my situation, he said it would be fine to drop the trailer off near the back of the store in the alley separating Ed's tires from the business next door. I felt a little nervous about leaving my brother-in-law's trailer in an alley, but I knew I had no other alternative other than staying the weekend. After parking the trailer near the back wall, I said a couple of protection prayers over the box on wheels and drove down the road towards Dateland using the old highway 80, which ran parallel to highway 8 from Wellton.

While driving on the old highway, one could see how the newer 8 took away a lot of roadside business from all the little farming communities existing in the desert from Gila Bend to Yuma. Few cars want to pull off for gas or eat in the local diners featuring the type of food found in the small communities. Some of the small towns do their best to attract the tourist or traveler passing by with large signs featuring petroglyphs from ancient Native American tribes who lived in the area many years before. The town just west of Gila Bend noted their location with a large sign stating, 'In the Middle of Nowhere'. A few curious travelers who always wanted to visit the 'Middle of Nowhere' might turn off, get gas at the country station, buy a few desert souvenirs and be on their way.

By now the sun was warming up and the shake at my ritualistic stop became the reward for a job well done. I wanted to get back to Phoenix so I ate trail mix and drank the shake while completing the last 90 minutes on the road. I pulled into Peoria and our apartment around 2:30 p.m. A return trip on Tuesday would be necessary to pick up the trailer with a new tire and return to New River where my brother-in-law's new house was located.

The weekend flew by and on Tuesday the drive to Wellton began early in order to be back in Phoenix by noon. When I arrived at Ed's tire the new wheel was already in place. All I needed to do was to hook up the trailer, pay the man and drive again to Dateland. After returning to Peoria, Suzanne and I quickly loaded the trailer and Blazer with anything left in the apartment and returned to New River. The cleaning crew would be arriving on Wednesday morning, followed by the carpet cleaner on Thursday and the final checkout with the leasing agent on Friday. We had moved out a month early but still needed to pay for June due to the year lease we had signed.

After the final checkout the weekend was spent with Suzanne in a small community called Cornville, located between Highway 17 and Cottonwood. She was house sitting for a friend in a beautiful home located on a couple of acres just outside the community center and country store. I needed to rest before the next trip on the eighth of June. I planned to go down to the Ranch for 10 days and start to organize the items in the house so it could be lived in. Propane would have to be hooked up, electricity changed into our names, and questions answered regarding the Internet and phone service on the Ranch.

June 8th came quickly, and I set off with the Blazer filled with boxes and articles I would need in order to live at the house. On this trip I decided to try the new border crossing near Mexicali. The San Luis guards knew me by now, and I was tired of paying a tax of which the amount was completely based on the whim of the agent checking the vehicle. The ritual shake-stop was made, and I found myself at the border around 11a.m. The woman guard spoke English and asked me what I had in the car and where I was going.

Telling a Mexican I was moving to San Felipe always brought an expression of amazement to their face. Again, the idea of Americans moving to Mexico, while so many Mexicans were trying to find their way north to work in the fields, homes, restaurants and hotels of all the border States seemed preposterous, to say the least. Her partner asked if I was carrying beer into Mexico and my answer was: "Why would I bring American beer into Mexico when Mexico makes better beer than many American beers. I like Negro Modelo the best. How about you?"

The custom guard laughed and probably could see I knew a little about good tasting beers. He seemed pleased I preferred Mexican beer instead of the mass-produced Budweiser or Coors beers. There are many smaller American beer companies that have begun making great beers again. They cannot compete with the big-named breweries that bring you every sporting event on television. They show hot chicks on sunny beaches drinking Bud or catching the Cool Train of Coors as it whips through town on the way to party bliss.

The woman guard and her partner waved me through without any inspection of the car and its contents. She probably said a silent prayer to some Saint to protect me in my move south of the border.

Gasoline Information: By now, the trip through Mexicali with stops at the currency exchange, gas station, and military post were becoming routine. I knew which exchange booth gave the best rates and which Pemex had the best price. Most of the gas is regulated, but I found the stations closer to the border have higher prices and those located further down the road toward San Felipe are a little cheaper. Months later I found out the real reason for the different gas prices in Mexico. My doctor in Brawley told me Mexico is divided up into three zones. Higher prices for gas are in the major cities where the income level for the population is at an elevated level. The lower prices for gas are in smaller communities like San Felipe because the wages are lower. The economic levels for communities set the gas prices. I now get enough gas in Mexicali for the drive to San Felipe where I fill up at a lower price per gallon.

Arriving at the Ranch in the afternoon allowed me plenty of time to unpack the car, put the bed mattress in place, make the bed and go to the local store for some dinner, and breakfast items. The house was filled with boxes dropped off on the previous two trips and nothing had been put away. My focus was to prepare a place to sleep, eat some dinner and dive into the job of putting the house in order the following morning. I slept lightly, waking up many times in the night. It was probably due to being overwhelmed and exhausted.

The morning started by making a pact with myself as to how many boxes I would attempt to unload each day. I needed to connect with the gas company to fill the tank outside the house and get Direct TV set up so I would have contact with the world beyond the border of Mexico. I also needed to find out how to get Internet in order to answer my e-mails. Posting to my friends on Facebook as to how the move was going and report any banditos along the road to San Felipe was important. Writing this book about my move to Mexico was also vital to me because it could help those who might be thinking of such a move. 'Learning to Love the Peso' could play a part in dispelling the fear-based beliefs concerning Mexico and the idea the country was a total war zone.

Z Gas: The gas company named Z gas was located in town and I needed to go there first. A friend who lived nearby told me I would not get gas for several days, because the company serviced residents north of San Felipe one day and homes to the south the next day. The visit to the office in town proved to be a different story. The woman behind the desk at Z gas made a quick call to one of the trucks servicing north of town. After seeing where he was located she told me he would be at my house in 20 minutes. Not wanting to wait for two more days I told her I would be there and headed back to the Ranch. I stopped quickly at a mercado for water and a few items to eat in the next few days. I arrived just as the Z gas truck was pulling into the guard station. I caught up with the vehicle and directed him to the house. Within 20 minutes the tank was filled.

This story proves a fact in Mexico. Residents who have lived on the Ranch for a while cannot predict when services will arrive. If the planets are in alignment, gas for your house can arrive quickly. I guess the higher power known by many different names throughout the world was smiling down upon me at that moment. I now had the gas to cook and heat things when needed.

Chapter 20
Starting to Settle In

Most of Thursday was spent looking for an attachment between the gas line and the stove after getting the gas tank filled. The attachment between the gas line and stove needed four trips to the hardware store. Because of my limited Spanish and the hardware store owner's lack of speaking English, getting the right part took time. The Z gas truck driver, who filled the gas tank, helped me find out why the stove would not fire up in the first place. Because it is a brand new house and I am the first to live in the new casa, the stove was never been hooked up to work. Many of the things that should have been working did not because the owner had not prepared the house for a renter. The stove still had a new gas line coming out from the back of it and the other gas line extended from the wall, with nothing to attach the two together.

Finding out where to go to get the needed attachment was an adventure only Mexico could give me. The Z truck driver spoke little English and my limited Spanish enabled me to pick up one or two words as to where I could find such an attachment. The driver had several deliveries to make and did not want to spend a lot of time trying to bridge the language gap between us.

I knew I did not want to live like this. Not being able to understand Spanish spoken by the driver of the Z gas truck was not acceptable. Lessons would start as soon as the house was in order. I could then sit on the porch with the peace of knowing the house was not full of unpacked boxes in every available space of the living room.

Around the time the driver handed me the bill of $1500 pesos for a full tank of gas (around 135 dollars), an American woman living in a nearby house showed up asking the driver in English if he had any more gas for another sale. Seeing a Z truck in the neighborhood awakens the nearby population to quickly run out to their gas tanks and see how much fuel is still in their containers. Fuel levels down to a quarter-tank would mean it is time to get more.

Without the means of cooking with flame, microwave dinners would have to be purchased and served until gas could be delivered. I know Trader Joe's in the States provides a wide range of culinary delights for the microwave oven, but the local mercado in town might be limited to ten different ways to heat up enchiladas using

Jose's secret sauce. On day three the meals might not be something to look forward to.

I was happy to see the woman. She seemed to be a retired resident in the neighborhood and I hoped she could help in the translation as to where I could buy the attachment between the stove and the gas line. When I asked her if she could translate for me and ask him where I could buy the needed hardware part, she turned to the driver and said, "Where can he buy the attachment he needs for the stove in the house?"

In my mind I started to laugh. I really was expecting her to speak Spanish to the Z driver. Instead she did what I could have done, speak English. She did not attempt to use any Spanish words at all, not even 'casa' for house. I do not know if she spoke any Spanish. At that moment I knew I was on my own as far as finding out where to go and find the needed part.

Language: My suggestion for the reader who may be thinking about going to a Spanish-speaking part of the world to retire or relax in a home or community is this: You need to at least try to learn some basic vocabulary for your survival in a foreign country. Words involving your house, car and food come to mind. At El Dorado the locals have told me that a woman comes over from Ensenada twice a year and teaches three weeks of intense Spanish classes to the residents. There are three levels taught. A pretest is given to place the potential student in the correct language class.

Wherever in Mexico or another Spanish-speaking country the reader might move, attempting to learn the language is a must if you want to integrate at all into the culture. I have found the residents will help you when you at least attempt to speak the language of their country. Also, learning a language has been listed as one of the best ways to combat memory loss. In a retirement community like El Dorado there are many such battles being fought.

One Task a Day: It took three trips to the local hardware store. I was finally able to locate the store because I did have some Spanish vocabulary in my arsenal. I was able to piece the needed words together. I also decided to try and complete three tasks in one day. I mention this fact because the reader needs to realize something. Living in a third-world-country or even one that may be on the verge of becoming a member of the "We have everything therefore we are modern" world of nations, means not everything can be accomplished in one day. For instance, going to the bank and shopping for food could take most of the morning. Ordering gas for the house and getting a part from the hardware store is not as easy as in the States, Canada or any European nation.

I needed to hook up to Direct TV. Dave, the man working in the El Dorado side of town, lived in a development on the way home. The information about Dave came to me via the owner of the Roadrunner Café. Summer was the slow season for those who serviced homes in the area due to many of the Snowbirds having left by the first of June. I was able to catch him at his house in Pete's Camp. He was able to come out and see where the satellite should go on the house and to give me a price of service.

By now the temperature of the day had reached into the 90's and I knew I was not going to get the dish and TV hooked up before sunset. I told Dave the next morning would work, when the temperature was still in the 70s and the sun was not burning down on the rooftop where he had to work to install the dish. Direct TV would bring me 300 plus stations, more than I ever had in the States, for only $45 a month. I had to purchase the dish and pay for installation, which amounted to $75. For a start up fee of $120 I could see more TV stations than I would ever need to see in a lifetime.

Before Dave left, I showed him my third attempt at purchasing the connection between the stove and the gas line. He spoke Spanish and said he would help me at the hardware store to try and find the correct part. We both drove to the store but after another round of digging through the limited number of valves in the store the owner suggested another store on the way to town. I thanked Dave for the help and set out to find the solution to the gas and stove problem.

I returned home in the evening after finding a second hardware store on the road into San Felipe. In this area where the Ranch is located, the Mexican entrepreneur finds a need for the inhabitants of an area and fills it. There are three stores near the Ranch selling home building supplies but the newly arrived local, me, has to find out where they are located from those who have been in the area for a while. There is no Home Depot sign on the road advertising the name we all recognize. Word of mouth is how one finds things in many third-world countries.

The second hardware store I was directed to was next to another mercado. The only evidence I could see that led me to believe I may be going to a hardware store were the sacks of cement and sand alongside a fence. The building was made of cement block. The store and building materials available for sale had a tall wire fence surrounding the compound. Poorer countries understand the need for guarding their investments and this hardware store was no exception.

As I walked into the establishment for the 'fix it yourself' owner, I knew right away I had found my future Home Depot. The place was filled with all the things one would need to maintain a house in Mexico in order to make life easier. The man behind the counter knew exactly what I needed, found it for me and as an added bonus, he spoke perfect English. I want to learn the local language but I needed the part now and Manuel had the answer for me in a language I understood.

When Dave arrived in the morning to install the TV dish I happened to mention the gas tank, just filled the day before and wondered how long he thought the amount would last. As we opened the lid to the tank a gas smell and hissing sound told us there was a leak in the line. Dave quickly shut off the valve to the tank. It had dropped 20 lbs of pressure overnight. We discovered the line from the tank to the house was only hand tight and the other end of the copper tube was cracked at the connection going into the house. I had TV, I went shopping for food and I filled the tank for the house but the job of fixing the gas line connection continued. For a house never lived in before there were many problems needing maintenance.

The next morning found me at the 'Casa Depot of El Dorado'. Again Manuel knew what I needed to fix my problem and sold me a flexible gas line from the tank to the connection going into the house. The job of connecting the line took five minutes and now I was really set up to do some serious cooking on the stove.

After being in the new house for two days, I awoke and turned on the stove to make my first coffee in the European coffee maker I have become addicted to. The brewer makes around two cups of the strongest, best-tasting coffee ever. Stronger coffee is made in Turkey but they are in a league of their own. The two cups of coffee I drink every morning gets me ready for the day.

I am now at the local Laundromat washing my several pairs of shorts and numerous tee shirts needed to complete my Baja wardrobe. I just return from a visit with Ed Jones, the info man.

He spends long hours on his computer updating residents and future residents on the changes coming to our community and how our HOA fees are being spent. He is invested in making the development the best it can be, and he serves on many of the committees getting the job done.

Information and News: A repeated tip I am giving the reader is to talk to those residents who are living in the area where you are thinking of moving. There will probably be a restaurant or bar attended by the local foreigners, and information of the latest changes is passed on to either the waitress who works there or the owner of the establishment. The owner could be an American or Canadian and gathering information and passing it on is an important part of why the business is so popular. We have one such dinner called the Roadrunner Café. I mentioned it earlier, and most communities will have such a place to go to and find out the latest news.

Internet Information: Man has a very unique way of getting around roadblocks in foreign lands and providing services no one thought possible. Internet is one example, and it seems to be the main concern of anyone thinking of moving to Mexico. I have been asked many times: "What is the Internet like? Can I get fast service and be able to watch videos on my computer? I have to be able to do my online investments. Are you sure the Internet is safe and secure in Mexico? I sure don't want someone hacking into my portfolio and taking my information."

These are valid concerns people have when taking the leap and moving to a third-world country. I have been visiting this development for the past six years. As I mentioned before every community of Americans and Canadians has one or two people who make it their business to know up-to-date information regarding questions like telephone service, Internet, television service and so on.

Experts in the field of computers may be living near you. There is an electronic store in San Felipe called San Felipe Technology Center. An American works there selling Internet satellite dishes and other devices, which enable good computer access. The laws have changed in Mexico and foreigners can own and operate a business in this country.

(2014 update) In the town of San Felipe there are businesses working on computers. For those on the Ranch the name Larry and Randy come to mind when service is needed for a PC. Larry lives on the Ranch and can be found most days at the water-volleyball game at the pool. Randy Kerr is in the neighborhood near the Ranch. His e-mail is randy@blueroadrunner.com

I also have met a young woman who works on Apple computers. Her name is Julie and her e-mail is (the.net.sf@gmail.com). SanFelipe.com.mx, is a site she promotes and she says, "we've always been the #1 Google result for "San Felipe" and we provide updated weather, news, road conditions, maps, and general information for the area."

El Dorado Ranch is now in the process of upgrading their telephone and Internet service to the residents. As the technology for this communication gets bigger the demand to improve service will happen in Mexico and other third world countries as well. Do not worry about not getting Internet where you move. There is a good chance it is already there and available due to the demand of the population living in the town or region. Mexico is being driven by the computer age like other third-world countries. Internet cafes can be found in many communities. The world is getting smaller through communication.

I finally found a good way to receive Internet. Telcel, the phone company, has an Internet stick which runs off the cell towers. When you purchase the stick you pay for how much service you want. Usually a month of 3G service runs about 500 pesos or around $38. If you are only going to be in Mexico for a couple of weeks and want service, you can pay for a week or two weeks at a time. One can recharge the service at any OXXO store by giving the attendant the phone number that comes with the stick and going to a Telcel store and have the service updated.

I was able to get a lot of help from a Mexican woman named Veronica at the Telcel store in San Felipe. I purchased the stick in Mexicali for less than the cost in San Felipe. I suggest if you are going to use an Internet stick, get the HUAWEI Mobile Broadband E153 white stick in a big city because it is a lot cheaper. Small towns have to purchase them and transport them to their towns. Telcel also sells another one, which was blue in color for a few pesos less but it did not work in my Apple 10.5.8. I think it works in a Leopard 10.6 or higher.

The computer, with the Internet has become the number one way people in Mexico communicate to friends within Mexico or in Canada and the

U.S. Sure there are cell phones for making any quick decisions about things like, "What shall I get for dinner, dear?" E-mail still seems to be the best way to keep up with each other for things not needing an instant decision such as: "George, are you and Peggy still coming by on Friday for a glass of wine and watch the sun set from the roof?"

"I am sure we still are. Peggy has her tennis game in the morning and I have my water volley ball game at the pool at noon. We will have a late lunch and set our TiVo to record our favorite show, which comes on while we will be watching the sunset with you. We should be there around 6 p.m."

I mentioned watching the sunset from the roof. For those of you who are not familiar with the style of houses built for the gringos, a roof room has become a popular addition to the living quarters of those who have great views of the ocean or mountains in or around the area of their development. A stairway goes up one side of the house, leading to the flat roof of the residence. One section of the roof usually has been tiled so that the inhabitants of the casa can go up for a view of the sunrise or sunset depending whether you live on the east coast or west coast of the Mexican mainland or Baja. In

El Dorado, we are located on the east coast of the seven hundred mile-long strip of land separating the Sea of Cortez from the Pacific Ocean.

Rooftop Information: Since I mentioned the roof top patio I think I need to expand on the extremes different residents go to in order to make the viewing areas of their homes suitable for their needs. The basic approach to using the upper floor is to bring up a few lounging chairs and maybe a patio table. Usually these items can remain in the cooler seasons with just a cover to protect them from wind or the occasional rain. Food and drinks can be brought up to the roof from the kitchen. After they are served they are brought back down to the main house. This is basic rooftop living 101.

The next level of rooftop dweller does not want to transport his prepared food and drink items up and down stairs. He added a gas line to the roof when he built the house so he can hook up his barbeque and cook those ribs and burgers while watching the sun set either over water or land depending upon where he lives. Drinks are usually kept in a small refrigerator, which is plugged into a wall socket. Power has also been added to this rooftop observation living room.

We are now entering the level of 'upper division' rooftop living.

The third level of rooftop dwelling has all the mentioned items but a few more have been added. A water line also goes up to the roof and a sink has been placed on the roof to wash any dishes used to make the party or viewing period a success. The dishes and cooking utensils are kept in a cupboard on the roof thus avoiding the need to carry them down the stairs to the main kitchen. The only thing I have not seen on the rooftop room is a small elevator used to transport any uncooked food items. Everyone living in this community who uses their rooftop needs to able to walk up and down stairs.

If the roof deck is needed during the day, an umbrella is handy to keep those who desire to be out of the direct sun safe from its burning rays. The rules pertaining to the development where we live has to do with permanent structures sticking up from the rooftops. Any roof structure blocking the view of the ocean or mountains from the house in front or behind your house is not allowed. In most areas a 15 ft. height limit of each house is mandatory and the properties are situated in such a way that the lots are staggered. Each house looks between the lots in front and back of where it is located. Every attempt is made to maintain the right of each home to see both the ocean and mountains from ground level.

Chapter 21
Return for One Last Load Plus a Wife

During the ten days I lived at the new home by myself, I was able to partly set up the kitchen, move all the boxes to the locations where the contents would soon live, and come to the realization the job would not be done in a short amount of time. Suzanne had completed her obligations of attending weddings, house-sittings and visiting all her friends in Flagstaff. She would be heading to New River and her brother's house on the 17th of June. I packed and drove to the border in the morning. Traveling the route now becoming familiar. The drive included filling up with cheaper Mexican gasoline near the border, waiting in line to cross, getting my ten-peso car wash and following the line of cars creeping towards the U.S. I still have not applied for a Sentri pass but all in good time.

I arrived in New River full of my routine food stops and a date shake. Suzanne came a few hours later and told me our close friends, Scott and Pam, were heading to the house to spend one last evening together before we made our way to Mexico and a lifestyle still alien to us. Scott arrived, soon after Suzanne and had to be directed to the house by telephone because country homes can be difficult to find.

"Take a right at the cactus in full bloom on the corner of the Roadrunner Bar and Grill. Go about a mile and keep an eye open for the Fire Station on your left. Turn right into the second driveway and the house is on the right. The neighbor has a huge American flag on his fence so you cannot miss it."

Scott drove into the driveway bringing a few bottles of a new beer he had discovered in his travels. With the heat starting to raise in the Phoenix area the beer went down easily and the effects helped to ward off the temperatures reaching their peak by the afternoon. When Pam arrived the beer was finished and we started to think where we should hold our 'going away' dinner. Anthem is a small community near New River, and the Italian restaurant located there became our choice for our last meal together for a while. Wine with dinner and going over wonderful memories we have shared together over the years completed the evening. Peru and Italy were just a few of the travel spots we shared, as well as my retirement dinner being held in a winery restaurant in Chianti. Even our waiter reminded me of my travels. He was from Vienna, Austria, the first foreign country I lived in from 1963 to 1964.

After the meal Pam and Suzanne were able to catch Starbucks to share their ritual drink. They drank coffee as a sacrament, while Scott and I still worshiped the date shake. With dinner and after-meal coffee completed, we headed back to the New River home. We set up the beds, turned on the fans, and waited for the desert to cool off as we tried to sleep.

In the morning, the last of our household items were packed in the Blazer, with a wicker chair tied onto the roof of the car. Every inch was filled. The final items put into the car were the clothes, which were laid on top of all the boxes so little damage to them could occur. There is nothing worse than having to iron all the clothes you own after driving 300 miles on a move. From Flagstaff, Pam had brought down some of Scott's famous (at least in our circle) Swedish pancakes, which were pre-cooked and just needed heating. After the meal the moment of departure was upon us. Pam and Suzanne shared tears while Scott and I shared bear hugs. Date shake drinkers only cry when they spill their drinks or at sad movies. After the Andersons were gone, we cleaned up and prepared for the day ahead.

Suzanne and I locked up the house and headed off to Phoenix for a few errands, which included getting things not available in San Felipe. Most of what we needed could be purchased in Mexicali where such stores like Home Depot, Lowes, Subway Sandwich and a variety of hotel chains have made their move across the border into the capital of Baja. We decided to get the items in Arizona and wait until our Spanish vocabulary increased to the level of being able to ask for what we needed without carrying around a Spanish-English dictionary.

Building Information: Here is a tip for the northern neighbor thinking of moving or having a house in the country of Mexico. The standard size windows in the states are not the same as the standard size windows in Mexico. I made all the measurements for eight windows in the house we were renting and we found only one pre-made curtain in any of the stores selling them. This concerned me at the time because I knew we needed the curtains to keep the blazing afternoon sun from heating the house like an oven.

The views in the morning were spectacular through the windows surrounding the dining room and kitchen. When the sun reached its peak in the sky and started the descent towards the western mountain range, the temperatures in July through September can bake bread in the desert. With most of the windows on the west side of the house, the heat could turn the dining room into a Gold's Gym sauna. We needed curtains and made a decision to stop in Yuma the following day, visit a material shop, and have the curtains made in San Felipe.

The homes in El Dorado and other gringo communities throughout Mexico find ways to block the intense heat increased by the glass in the windows. Porches are commonly found on the fronts and backs of the houses. Many residents have added large blinds in the areas of the patio where the afternoon sun comes through the windows and into the house. The views are temporarily blocked until just before sunset. The beauty of the mountain range again returns with the lifting of the blinds between 7:00 and 7:30 p.m. in the summer, and the early evening desert can be viewed from inside the house or from the rooftop living quarters. Most of the residents use the top of their house patios in the months following summer. The reason the sun sets so early where we live is due to the 10,000 ft mountain range directly behind San Felipe and the Ranch.

Our final stop was in Goodyear near Phoenix where old friends of mine, Joe and Michelle, now lived after moving to Arizona in 2004. During the seven years they lived in the Phoenix area, we were in Flagstaff and never connected. Only 140 miles separated us but the distance probably was more psychological than physical. They purchased a house in a beautiful foothill community, sold their Santa Rosa house when the market was good in California, and purchased a much larger home in Arizona before the housing boom happened and shot prices skyward throughout the state. During our year in Peoria, we re-connected and got together several times for lunch and dinner. I still had not visited their home in Goodyear and we were now going to stay the night with them before becoming expats in the country only 75 miles south if you are a bird or 100 miles if you drive.

Our evening with Joe and Michelle included remembering old stories of when we met in 1986, singing in the New Thought Church together in Santa Rosa, and the coupling of Joe and Michelle, with me being in their wedding in the late 80s and Joe in my wedding with Suzanne in 1992. We still kept in touch, but with our move to Arizona in 2000, we lost contact with many friends in Santa Rosa including Joe and Michelle. It was great seeing them in their beautiful home and their beautiful daughter Jenna, now 17, last seen by me in 2000 just before our move to Arizona. A drive around the large housing development where they lived, accompanied with a home-cooked meal and an evening in the living room gave Suzanne and me the needed break. Our rushing-around day was over and tomorrow was our final push towards the border.

The home of my friends was decorated with Southwest art, including sculptures and wall hangings with the colors including every shade found in the Sonoran Desert. This desert stretches from Arizona down into Baja where we lived, and the only difference was the average rainfall. The Phoenix area received more moisture than its Mexican counterpart, and a larger variety of vegetation could be found in Goodyear. Pictures of old friends from Santa Rosa were in the pool table room and it brought back more memories of our singing and friendship together in Sonoma County.

Along with comfortable living quarters in their home, the life-style both Joe and Michelle created demonstrated their ability to work well together. Michelle was a graphic designer and still had clients in her field. Both were now starting a book publishing business helping independent writers, who choose not to use the large publishing houses, to get their story out to the world. The 'in home' office on the second floor looked like a well-tuned Mercedes Benz with computers and schedules completing the working quarters. They both seemed happy in the life they had created together. Michelle loved the desert heat while Joe longed for the cooler months starting in October, so it was best to question him about life in Arizona starting in the fall.

By 9:00 Suzanne and I knew we needed sleep and made our exit to the guest room. Sleep came quickly and the morning even quicker. Fruit, cereal, yogurt and coffee started our engines for the day. We climbed into the Blazer around 10:00 a.m. and headed down the road. The journey to Mexico by now could be completed with my eyes closed. The reader should know where our first stop was made before reaching Yuma. Suzanne is not a date-shake groupie and Starbucks has not opened a store in Dateland yet. While I was ordering my drink of the Road Gods she picked up a few snacks. She has a metabolism needing nourishment every two hours and a little trail mix usually did the job.

Yuma has a Starbucks, and it is located right next to a Subway sandwich store. We had lunch after buying the needed curtain material at Jo Anne's across the street. The young girl who waited on us was so helpful and patient, I felt the need to write a complimentary note to the main office. She was young and already a store manager, and from the helpful way she guided us through the process of measuring and cutting, I can understand how she has risen to the rank of manager. We crammed the material into the only open space left behind the driver's seat and drove off to the new border crossing at Mexicali.

This crossing, like the one I made on June 8, involved no taxes for articles being brought down to San Felipe. After telling the border guard we were moving to El Dorado Ranch, he simply waved us on and only peeked into the car from the outside windows.

Border Crossing Information: My tip for the reader at this time, based upon my experience of taking items for our house across the border, is this: The east border crossing into Mexico at

Mexicali seems to be the most lenient. Had I crossed at this border with the trailers I may have been able to continue without paying a tax on my household items. The Mexican authorities in Mexicali seem to understand the articles are for my house and there is no need to trouble me with inspections and other time-consuming negotiations as to how much the tax will be. The only thing they are looking for is new items purchased in the States. These purchases usually have an import tax. How to avoid such a duty is to remove the new item from the box in which it was purchased. Remove any sales tags. I am not promoting this behavior. It is up to the individual making such a move to attempt this approach or not. I do not know if there is a harsh penalty for tax evasion because I have not tried it. Used items are not taxed so it is up to the reader as to what they want to do.

Making the move to Mexico as easy as possible for the northern Yankee is a positive benefit for Mexico. The residents living south of the border spend a lot of money. Evidence of foreign companies investing and putting their stores in the capital of Baja Norte can be seen with a drive through the city. More businesses are moving to Mexico to have their products made and then sold in the States. Solar companies from the States are having their product made south of the border in order to compete with the low cost of solar panels made in China. Where this is all heading, I do not know. Maybe in ten years the American worker will be trying to sneak across the border to work in the Mexican factories making things for the American population. How would that be for a reversal of the situation we face today?

Gas, money exchange and a bathroom break are now completed and we are on the 5 heading south. I tell Suzanne about the progress on the road construction further down towards San Felipe and that the side roads are still bumpy. She usually finds a pillow and sleeps through the rough ride around the construction zones. We negotiate the detours and soon are pulling up to the last military stop located about 20 miles from El Dorado Ranch. A quick inspection of the car and we are soon at the house on the Ranch. We are met with the piles of boxes I placed near the locations where they will be unpacked and put away in the coming days.

Chapter 22
Overwhelm

Moving Information: The date is June 19, 2011. The tip to pass on to readers wanting to move to Mexico or at least to the Sonora Desert is this: Try to do the transition in the cooler months. Our situation dictated when we needed to come to Mexico based on the year lease we had signed with the apartment in Peoria.

Having transported our last load of items for the house in Mexico, we are now here. The brand-new casa had never housed a resident before. The bed was made and enough items remained in the refrigerator to put a meal together. We unloaded the back of the Blazer and added to the boxes scattered throughout the house. We were totally committed to being in Mexico with everything we owned with us.

At this point in time I had already spent ten days living in the house, unloading boxes and moving things around. The TV was set up, gas tank filled, stove working and air conditioning in three of the four locations pumped lifesaving cool air. The things waiting to be fixed were the shower in the master bathroom, fan in the living room, air conditioning split in the living room and a strange smell coming from the master bathroom.

The agent, who represented the owner, knew about these problems. He explained to me they could be related to the house having been empty for two years without anyone ever living in it. A house, like a person, has to use all their parts or deterioration sets in. The owner even dropped by for a visit with the year lease to sign and to view the trouble areas in the house. She was from Glendale, AZ, a suburb of Phoenix, located next to Peoria. She seemed pleased someone had rented the house because now she had some income while the market remained low in Mexico as well as in the States.

We were both living in the house and the problems still existed. Getting things done in a timely manner based on how things are done in the States is not something one should expect in Mexico. Another e-mail was sent to the agent. We did not have a phone yet. The agent dropped by in the morning promising to bring Oscar who owned the Fix It Express, a company servicing many of the homes on the Ranch.

Oscar arrived with the agent the next afternoon on his way back from getting supplies in Mexicali and was shown the different problems throughout the house. When he came to the master bathroom with the shower not working and a smell coming from somewhere, he was able to fix both of those problems within five minutes. He simply removed the showerhead, took out his pocketknife and cleaned out the mineral buildup clogging the outlet. Because the house sat for so long without use the water trapped in the head had evaporated leaving deposits found in the water. The leftover buildup caked the shower holes completely, allowing only a drop of water to pass through.

Mexican House Information: With the shower working, Oscar explained the smell in the bathroom would also be fixed. He explained how the house, because it had not been used for so long, lost the water in the trap below the shower due to evaporation. The smell from the septic was coming up through the water lines. With water again in the water lines and filling the trap, the smell could no longer come up through the shower drain.

Oscar said he would return the next morning with a man and fix the AC unit in the living room. The fan located in the same room had been fixed by myself the day before. The reader needs to know an important tip when dealing with houses constructed in Mexico. Unless you are sitting in the same room when the electrician is wiring the fans, lights or any other device needing a switch to turn it off or on, the place where one might expect a power source to be does not necessarily mean it will be there. If you are sitting in the room and tell the electrician you want the switch to the fan and the switch to the light to be located on the same wall, he will do so. If not, he may put the switch for the fan on one wall and the power for the light on another wall. This was the case of the fan not working in the living room. Its power switch was located on another wall completely opposite from the light source. I just happened to be going around the house one day trying all the different switches and came across the living room fan switch located near the entrance to the master bedroom. The reasoning behind such a decision, when left to a worker, seems to be best explained by this statement:

"What is the problem? The power is connected to all the devices. You just need to memorize which switches go to which device or mark them with a piece of tape. There is no problem here. Welcome to Mexico."

An adventure is found around very corner in Mexico and you are never bored.

I have a friend on the Ranch whose wife sat inside their house when it was under construction for the wiring and finish work. She brought her lunch and placed herself in a chair, directing the workers to do exactly what she wanted, done during the final stages of the interior finish work. The friend also told me the builders are fair and will redo the job if it is not what the owner wanted and usually with no added cost. If you have a good builder, and there are several with good reputations in the San Felipe area, you will end up with the house of your dreams, and usually more house than you owned in the States.

Air Conditioning Information: The house, after Fix It Express completed their work, now had all four AC units working. This meant we could be cool in all the areas of the house where we were working or living. The AC units, different from cooling found in the States with central air sending cool breezes to all the rooms at once, are called splits. Each room has a separate cooler on the wall leading to an independent AC unit on the roof. Usually the bedrooms have small size systems in place and the larger living areas have the bigger AC units mounted on the wall to cool the larger spaces. Electricity in Mexico is a valued luxury and the idea of cooling only the area where you work or live is an energy-saving system, found in almost all the houses in the community where we live. I remember seeing only one house in Phoenix using this system with all other homes utilizing central heating and cooling. To shut down a room in Mexico not being used, the occupant of the house just needs to close the door.

Suzanne and I started unpacking boxes the next day after our arrival. It was now June 20 and the longest day of the year, plus the higher temperatures and humidity would soon follow. I explained to Suzanne the need to pace ourselves and set a time to stop each day. After we cleaned up we went to the ocean or pool to relax and check our e-mail using the Wi-Fi at the Ranch office or poolside.

Self Doubt: I remember when I first came down on June 8 that I really started to doubt what I had done by making the move to the Ranch and Baja. I woke up on day four and looked out over the desert surrounding the house and said to myself, "Shit, what have I done?"

There seems to be a pattern here, and this could be marked as another tip to the reader. At some point, probably within the first week of a move when you find yourself with all your belongings in a country completely different from what you know, you may wake up feeling overwhelmed and disoriented. There is no Starbucks down the road to greet you before breakfast or a Harkins Theater with 20 screens giving you the latest film, which opened on Friday. There are not fifteen different restaurant chains starting with Olive Garden and ending with The Elephant Bar.

There are attempts by both Mexican and American businesses to bring you something similar to an American breakfast or espresso coffee but the malls and 'get anything you want at any time' lifestyle was now 100 miles to the north. For those communities further into Mexico, hundreds of miles lay between them and the border and the land of 'Too Much Good Stuff'. In the highly developed tourist areas on the southern tip of Baja, accommodations and food items used by the Americans and Canadians are found because money can purchase just about anything and have it delivered to your community.

By day three the feeling of, 'What am I doing here?' hit Suzanne.

She never lived in another country before, let alone a third-world country where they speak a language of which she only knows a few words. The title of this chapter is 'overwhelm' and I am sure most of those who have made such a move and change in their living arrangement have felt this emotion. For the next three days Suzanne did her best to unpack boxes, arrange the house in a workable fashion and find her place in a community of Americans. Many have lived at least two years or more at the Ranch.

When she could go no further setting up the house she spent time crying, while sitting in her chair in the bedroom. She was homesick for all her friends and the lifestyle she had left behind. Her vegetarian eating habits were looked upon as an anomaly in the community and she did not have much interest in the many card games and domino groups found on the entertainment calendar.

About 85% of the Ranch residents leave for the summer and only the hardcore year-round homeowners remain. Most of these have found a niche for themselves and developed a routine to get them through the day.

Water volleyball usually took care of the ex-jocks on the ranch and a daily appearance at the pool, sporting deep tans, Fu Manchu mustaches and the desire to have fun rounded out their day. After playing a series of round robin games the team with the most wins would be declared champs for the afternoon. Some of these water jocks lived in the solar sections of the Ranch and the pool gave them the needed relief to get through the heat of the summer. A cold beer numbed the evenings of warm air being moved around by the fan in their living rooms while watching the sports channel. Few residents in the solar section have enough batteries to operate an AC unit, so the fan is their only relief.

Ex-jocks at pool getting ready for water volleyball

Tennis courts and a golf course offered other country club sports, but only in the early times of day could these forms of exercise be attempted during the summer months. The fall through spring seasons allowed tournaments to be held, along with another game called pickle ball, developed back in 1965 and named after the dog of the person who started the sport.

Eventually Suzanne got past her period of loss and went through a few days of soul-searching. She realized how dependent she was to all the 'stuff' offered in the States and she was now determined to discover why she ended up living in Mexico. Her strong belief in a guiding force, which many westerners call God, told her she was sent to live here for a reason and she needed to discover what it was. It seemed to me she was now on a spiritual quest to find her place in a community of Canadians, Americans and Europeans, many wanting to give their lives more meaning by giving back to the Mexican community just down the road. Her interest in the animal shelter, which neutered and spayed stray dogs and cats in order to cut back or eliminate homeless animals, inspired her. She was willing to visit the shelter and see where she was needed to help in some way.

As soon as the house reached a stage of order, with the master bedroom and living room cleaned up and the kitchen void of any unpacked boxes, the feeling of overwhelm began to dissipate. Suzanne is a Libra. The symbol for this astrological sign is a woman holding a scale. Order and balance in the life of anyone born under this sign is most important and needed in their life in order to function on earth. The kitchen and living room were always kept in a clean and neat condition during our previous 19 years of marriage. I needed to pick up after myself and keep my mess in an enclosed area out of sight from any visitors who may drop by.

People like me, born under the sign of Aquarius, can live with a mess much more easily. We clean up but not every day.

Medical Information: After about a week of being here we started to make plans to drive up to El Centro in California. The locals call the trip a 'dash to the border'. Another tip for the reader thinking of a Mexico life style is this: Communities existing within a few hundred miles of the States can still maintain access to the medical doctors and services there. The lack of medical help by an American doctor is a major concern for many wanting to live south of the border. I have met Americans living in developments three days drive south into Mexico. These communities may or may not have a good medical team in their area. This should be a part of the research one needs to do before choosing a new home in Mexico. In El Dorado there is an insurance one can obtain for helicopter transport to a hospital in the states. Such a service places the patient within an hour of needed help.

Along with the many questions asked of the long-term residents in our community, Suzanne and I found out a clinic existed in the town of Brawley, a short drive north of El Centro. We needed to transfer our medical files from

Phoenix to the clinic and make an appointment to meet our new doctors. A medical doctor is located on the Ranch property for yearly checkups and smaller emergency needs. Prescriptions and other forms of help might need a gringo doctor in California. This is true if one uses Medicare to get medications and have yearly check ups.

The stay in El Centro would take two days. The medical transfers and paper work were completed on day one and a shopping spree on day two. Vacation Village, a hotel just off highway 8 in El Centro, became our overnight destination. Because many people from the Ranch do the 'dash to the border' and want to stay for a night, the motel offered a discount for El Dorado residents. Forty-five dollars included a breakfast in the morning and two drink tickets in the sports bar located next to the office. We checked in and headed north to Brawley to start our medical paper work.

Questioning people on the street in Brawley eventually directed us to the local medical facility. We were not sure if we were given the same facility those on the Ranch used, but it was the one the locals used. We finally arrived at Clinicas de Salud Del Pueblo, Inc. and began the process of finding out how to get our records moved from Phoenix to Brawley. A helpful receptionist greeted us at the window. She made the experience a true delight. We were able to fill out the transfer papers from the records department, book an appointment in two weeks, and get directions to an eye doctor. We completed this within forty-five minutes.

Brawley and El Centro are towns consisting of a high percentage of Hispanic Americans. Everywhere we went, Spanish was spoken as a first language among the workers and inhabitants. Friendliness was another trait we discovered in the area. The clinic, eye doctor and The Dollar Tree across from the eye doctor's office seem to bend over backwards wanting to help us in anyway they could.

This part of California felt like a transition from Mexico in a way I can only try to describe. The locals were all Americans but with ties to the country just to the south. It felt like I was in Mexico but with everything a lot cleaner. The visible trash in towns and cities south of the border is the biggest obstacle for me. The sidewalk and streets are kept up in the States and storefronts are in much better condition. Third-world countries seem to have a different outlook on trash. The municipal governments probably do not have enough revenue in their budget to operate a good trash pickup system. Lack of repairs to the inner structure are also noticeable in Mexico where the cities of Calexico, El Centro and Brawley seem to have more tax revenues to keep those areas of their cities up to date. The large box stores are located in El Centro including Wal-Mart, Vons and Home Depot. These stores accepted our business the next day before heading back to San Felipe.

Stockpiled with items not found in our small village of San Felipe, we decided to cross the border and go through the central part of Mexicali. We exchanged money and gassed up. Even though the price of fuel in the States started to drop, the Mexican cost of filling the car remained lower. $3.00 for a gallon of regular gas seemed to be holding. With the Mexican government controlling all the fuel prices in the country, the cost would continue to remain lower than in the States.

Several years had passed since our last drive through the capital of Baja. I mentioned before that the large international chain businesses like Home Depot, Lowe's, Subway and Holiday Inn (Fiesta Inn) have started to find their way into the high-population areas of Mexico. We drove past many of these box stores and decided to visit them on our next trip and do some price comparisons. Items sold would be in pesos and all we needed to do was convert currencies and see which side of the border offered the better deals.

The drive back to the Ranch was becoming routine for me. The only change happening on the road was the construction of drainage pipes and tunnels being placed under highway 5. As more of the project became completed, the crew seemed to be moving towards San Felipe in the government's preparation for the 'Great Flood'. The side roads, which cars had to take while on their return to San Felipe or trip to the border, changed on each trip. Any person returning from California would be questioned regarding the roadwork and the length of the drive on the dusty route around the construction area.

Chapter 23
Finding Our Place

Once the boxes in the main areas of the house were put away and the pictures hung on the walls, the living arrangements were completed. A routine was established to help us survive the summer heat. Suzanne is a daily walker. To continue this practice she woke up before sunrise, dressed and got out on the roads winding through the neighborhood before the heat arrived. I have committed to going with her every other day but my walking legs have not been used for a while. The length of my stroll is about half of her trek. The swimming pool in the early mornings is crowded. A new pool complex being built on the mountainside includes one pool designated for lap swimming; I may have a future in swimming again.

Most developments in Mexico are going to have many types of activities on the calendar. The reasons events are held for the people living in developments amount to two main ones. Many of the items on the list are card games or different types of domino challenges. Mental stimulation and keeping the mind sharp is a concern for most of the inhabitants, who seem to average in the mid 60's. Along with the calendar games, splinter groups have formed for those who want to play cards 24-7 and try to do so.

The social contact is the second reason for the need of an events calendar. Because Suzanne and I are new to the Ranch the process of getting to know your neighbors and other residents can be somewhat challenging. Right now the population of the development is down to 15% of normal due to many of the snowbirds and seasonal residents being gone. The activities do not have as many participants, so instead of twelve tables of six players at each table, only one or two tables attract enough individuals who spend the afternoon together playing, staying cool and visiting.

Summer Heat: Summers in Mexico can be warm and expensive, with air conditioning units blazing most of the day. If you ever held a wish to visit Canada or the New England section of the States, summer is the time to do so. We plan to be here most of the summer with a few trips to California. Next year could bring us back to the Pacific Coast, visiting friends, family or just staying with Tom Bodett who says he will "leave the light on for us". All we would have to do before leaving Mexico is this. Shut off the electricity, turn off the gas line and lock up for the summer. Neighbors staying for the warmer months can water any plants one may have in the patio. Such a deed is repaid when they leave for a vacation or trip and you are around to water their plants. Gardening services also exist and are conducted by residents who live all year on the Ranch and earn a little extra money managing yards.

Many developments also have activities for the outdoor and more physical retiree. I have met several younger couples who were able to sign off from the workforce by the age of 55. Police and firefighters are well paid during their careers, and if they start at age 25 and put 30 years into their jobs, they usually end up with a good pension and remain fit, partly due to the type of job they held for 30 years.

The few such residents I have met fitting into this category. They have large garages full of all types of equipment needed to maintain their off road vehicles. Driving deep into the mountains or desert is one of their main hobbies. Baja is famous for going off-road and far into the backcountry.

Most of these off-road groups demand each of the drivers in the clubs to have a GPS device with them. Getting lost in Baja in an area of desert with no means of locating where you are or contacting anyone for help could have only one outcome. If by chance your body is recovered the nearest hill might be named after you and one of those wooden crosses, like those found along the highways of Baja and Mexico, would be placed near where the remains were found. In other words, be careful when touring the backcountry. Safety is always important.

Besides all the activities we can engage in, there is still the chore of finding which phone system to use and how to get Internet at one's house. Skype is used by a lot of residents and allows them to talk to their children and see how big the grandkids are getting. All these things take time to set up, and talking to residents in the neighborhood can produce different answers to the same question.

Today is July 7 and tomorrow marks the day I have lived in Mexico for a month. Yesterday and the day before were spent waiting around the house for the Fix It Express business to arrive and get the refrigerator working again. For the past few weeks the cold side of the two-door refrigerator has slowly been loosing its ability to keep food cool. The freezer side seems to work fine. Several e-mails to the rental agent explaining the loss of this most-needed appliance drew action with the promise of the crew to be here on Tuesday between 10:30 and 11:30. We still have not purchased a phone to use for local calls. I blame such lack of interest in obtaining the device on other priorities. Unpacking, trying to get Internet service, adjusting to the heat and humidity and our continued questioning of the long time residents as to which phone to get, tops our list. By 2:30 the Fix It crew still had not arrived. The need to drive to the pool and check our e-mail as well as cool off became more important than waiting for the work team.

The next morning, after getting up with Suzanne and doing my alternate day of walking and then finding something to write about in order to get my 1000 words added to the book each day, I headed into the small community near the Ranch where the local mercado sold food and filtered water. We were low on water and the local agua had to be filtered to remove the minerals and other agents too heavy for the human body. I usually do not go to the store at 8:00 a.m. and I was surprised at what I found. The man who cooks and bakes for the deli in the store had just put out his early morning supply of gourmet pastries including American donuts, apple turnovers (my favorite), and a few special breads such as banana and whole wheat. Several long time residents were sitting and enjoying the fresh out of the oven delights and they seemed to have made this their 'satisfy the sweet tooth' stop.

After filling the water containers and picking up a few fresh fruit items for the morning cereal at home, I returned to the rack of fresh baked items. I placed my hand over my favorite junk food and felt the heat still rising from this culinary wonder. This was no ordinary apple turnover. It measured almost a foot in length, contained so many apples that the contents were oozing out of the slits on top, and there were at least a dozen deserts on the cooling racks. I knew the flaky crust had to be from an American recipe because I had never seen anything like this in any Mexican panaderia in town. For 20 pesos or around $1.50 the closest thing to an authentic American apple turnover was going to make it into my mouth and be eaten before I returned home with water and fruit. Had these early morning delights been made in the States the local police force would have discovered them by now and would have at least cleaned out the donut rack by 8 a.m.

Appliances Information: I drove home eating the evidence of my morning sweet tooth addiction and throwing away the container before entering the house. I decided to drive to the home of Henry, our rental agent, and his wife Charlotte to report the 'no-show' of the Fix It Express crew the day before. A few phone calls and the team promised they would be at our home within an hour. Remembering I was in Mexico I set my mental timer for two hours before expecting them. While visiting Charlotte she asked if we had purchased a washer and dryer yet. I said no. We were thinking of a basic set I had seen on my last trip to Home

Depot. She suggested on our next visit to stop by Arizona Mills and visit the Sears outlet. She explained to me a good set of slightly damaged washer and dryer (scratched or small dent) could be purchased there and brought down for less money than anything purchased in Mexicali. Her only warning was to remove the items from the containers they may be in and make sure no price tags could be found on the items.

Crossing at Mexicali would also improve my chances of not having a tax for new items placed on the appliances. I had found out at a social event the week before that the pesos I paid at the San Luis border crossing were bribes. Mexico does not place a tax on used items coming into their country. Had I known this, I would have crossed at Mexicali with the trailer-load of items and never paid a cent. I still felt fortunate to have only paid a total of 600 pesos or around $55 for all the articles brought into Mexico and not the two first bribes of $900 or $75 per trailer.

When the crew for the refrigerator arrived after 90 minutes, they set to work trying to figure out how the cooler only worked on the freezer side and not the cooler side. We set the freezer to a setting of 1 and moved all the items not able to survive without the cold into the freezer side. We had an operating refrigerator on the freezer side and nothing on the refrigerator side. I could see this arrangement was messing up the workings of the icebox because snow was accumulating on the back of the freezer and this was not normal. Two hours later the crew finished replacing parts to the refrigerator, cleaned up their mess and said they would return with the needed parts for the stove.

By 1:30 the crew had not returned and we felt no change in the refrigerator side where most of our food items now sat. We decided to do our routine pool visit, check e-mail and let the rental agent know the situation before we left the house. On our return around 5 p.m. a note on the door told us Henry had returned with the crew. The note said the stove part had to be ordered and to give the refrigerator more time to cool off. He said if there was no change by morning then we should call and get the team to return once more and attempt to get the most-needed item in a household in Mexico to work. We were done for the day and headed to bed around 9:00 p.m.

The next morning I awoke feeling skeptical, really not wanting to open the refrigerator. I was sure there would be no change. I was wrong. The water for drinking was cold and all the items needing a cooler temperature in order to survive were enjoying themselves on the shelves away from the heat of the Baja summer.

When Oscar, the owner of Fix It Express, dropped by later in the morning to fix the stove he explained to us a fact about refrigeration in warm weather.

"It takes about seven hours for a unit to cool off and start working properly," he said.

We thanked him for doing a good job and within an hour he and his worker replaced the gas outlets or O-rings in the center of each burner with a smaller size. Another interesting fact when getting appliances to work properly is to know what type of gas is being burned in the stove. Natural gas needs a large opening in the burner and propane gas only needs a small outlet. We use propane in Mexico but the O-rings in the stove were for natural gas. The flame was so high we could have cooked marshmallows and made S'mores each night for dinner on the open stove. The only setting possible was the lowest and even at low the cooking pans became blackened by the higher mixture of oxygen with the propane. The stove now emitted a low flame. Things take longer to cook but then again we are retired and have time to watch the cactus grow so the lower flame is fine for now.

Cell Phones: The purchase of a local cell phone became another milestone, and we have now added another $50 to the richest man in the world's money bin. Carlos Slim owns Telcel. We now can call to order things like water and gas from the suppliers in town instead of driving seven miles into San Felipe and placing the order. After a month of questioning the locals regarding their phones, we decided to get one cell phone for all local calls in the area and purchase minutes each month. We have no idea how many we need to purchase and the phone, made by Samsung, comes with a 100 minutes starting chip.

Buying the right amount of phone time can be a real balancing act, especially when one first arrives at their new home in Mexico. We know only a few people in the area and only use the phone to order services. More minutes can be purchased and special deals are given to those phone users who need to make a lot of calls. These minute deals come and go all the time, so there is no point in giving the reader today's special, but I will give an example. If you purchase 400 minutes in the month of July, the phone company adds another 200 minutes for free. In other words, the more minutes added to the phone, the more extra time is given to the user at no extra cost.

Another note to the reader regarding phones in Mexico is this: Ed Jones told me the Nokia phones were the only ones having the ability to give the user instructions in English on programming the phone. Since then I have seen many phones used by Ranch residents and they seem to have figured out how to use their devices, even though they are not made by Nokia. When we purchased our Samsung phone there was a section in the applications where the user could use English for help and instructions. It seems the other companies in Mexico are seeing the need for their phones to have a choice as to which language the owner may use to complete any transactions.

American cell phones: American cell phones need to have the data sections of the device turned off when coming into Mexico for a visit. Internet access is OK to leave on, but the new phones continue to download information even when you are not using it. The phones will charge high fees because you are in Mexico, a foreign country, and international charges kick in. Visitors to Mexico have received $500 phone bills when they return to the States because the data-downloading devices on their phone continued to work at exorbitant rates.

When we return to the states next week, our plan is to contact an AT&T store and sign up for one of the 'Call Mexico' plans. I have been told the story of how such a plan came into existence. Previously Mr. Slim and his Telcel phone company held the monopoly on such a plan for users to call Mexico from the States or vice versa. He came up with the idea because of the many Canadians and Americans living in his country who where paying high rates to, as E.T. put it, "Phone home."

AT&T purchased the rights to use this idea, knowing such a large population of Americans, Canadians and Mexicans needed to communicate to friends and relatives south of the border and those living in Mexico, north of the border. I do not know what Mr. Slim called his plan, (probably something on the order of 'Call a Gringo') but here is how the plan works today: AT&T is the only company with this plan. They bought the rights from Mr. Slim and pay him a large check each month for use of his original idea. Telcel no longer offers their international plan and gets paid by AT&T who does all the work keeping the service up and running. Now I am starting to see why Mr. Slim is the richest man in the world.

WATER

I felt the need to give this subject a special heading due to the importance of it if the reader has chosen to live in a dry area of Mexico. El Dorado Ranch is located in the Sonoran Desert, the same desert that stretches down from Phoenix thru Yuma and further south of San Felipe. A mountain range cuts through the middle of Baja separating the Pacific Ocean side and preventing almost all the storms in the winter from reaching the Sea of Cortez and the Sonoran Desert. In the summer, large thunderstorms accumulate over the Pacific and make their way towards the Sea of Cortez. The 10,000 ft. peak, Mt. Diablo and the smaller surrounding mountains block the clouds and cause them to climb in altitude and drop their moisture. Rain can be seen by the residents in San Felipe and surrounding areas as it falls on the peaks, just a few miles to the west of town.

The Pacific storms in the winter do the same thing. They reach the mountain range and because they are forced to rise in their attempt to clear the peaks the moisture is dropped and little rain, if any, reaches the sandy desert to the east. What does happen to all this moisture is this: Cascades of water make their way down the mountains to the west and to the east. All the water flowing east pours into a lakebed and is absorbed into the dry earth, creating a giant aquifer under the ground and hidden from the intense summer heat of the Baja sun. The water amount, I am told, is vast, and a pipeline has been laid from the underground water into San Felipe where it is collected and sold at an inexpensive rate. The abundance of water allows the price to remain low.

The above scenario is the reason El Dorado and other developments have sprung up along the beachfront coastline of Baja. An unlimited water supply is as valuable as the gold mine located 25 miles north of El Dorado ranch. Developments such as those found in Rocky Point located on the mainland almost straight across from San Felipe have a big water problem. The hotels being built along their shoreline have to build and operate a desalination system to convert the seawater into drinking water. The cost of such a system can be expensive, and the expense is usually passed on to the consumer as an added cost of living in the area.

I needed water for my cistern and I called Oscar of Fix It Express. This man has a reputation of trying to fill all the needs of North Americans on the ranch by providing almost everything they need. He builds homes, maintains any house problems they may have, and delivers water to the houses with cisterns. The house we are renting has a water cistern built to hold 1500 gallons of water. The water truck delivering the water is around 2500 gallons of water. When I called for the water to be delivered I guessed as to how much water remained in the tank. Oscar thinks I probably had a few hundred gallons still in the tank because I only used ¾ of the truck's capacity. I still had to purchase the total amount in the truck and Oscar said he would dump the excess water onto any plants or area surrounding the house. We are in a rental, and the only plants surrounding the house included ocotillo, palo verde trees and a type of pipe organ cactus found throughout the desert.

Dumping the remaining water on the surrounding vegetation would have upset the survival cycle they were used to. This being the dry season, all the plants are probably in some type of shut-down mode conserving their energy until the two to three inches of rain makes its way into the Sonoran desert during the winter months. At that time, if the rains are plentiful enough, the ocotillo will leaf and bloom and the palos verde may produce a flower, which attracts some type of desert bee to its pollen. The bees return home somewhere underground. Next time I get water I will let my neighbor know and have any remaining agua put into his tank or grey-water system from which he waters his vast plant population covering his backyard and front porch.

Neighbors' seem to watch out for each other in this community and in other communities throughout Mexico. We speak the same language and draw our collectiveness from our cultural upbringing, and the need to watch each other's backs remains a strong theme repeated over and over again at the social gatherings I have attended. Watching out for each other is not from an "Us vs. Them" stance but more from an information and knowledge position. Those who have lived here for a few years already experienced the learning curve I am now facing.

Our neighbor's house (Suzanne and Ed)

An example of such a scenario happened the next day after the water was delivered. My neighbor, Ed, dropped by to give Suzanne, my wife, a note from Suzanne, his wife, regarding the service both were performing in town at the ZAPP clinic. I mentioned to him the water delivered yesterday filled my cistern and about 1000 gallons remained in the truck. I told him next time I got water he could have any amount remaining in the truck. I knew he had a grey-water tank in his backyard for the plants. He also had room in his cistern unless he had just filled up the day before as well.

Ed said he would buy any amount left over. He also asked me how much I paid for the water. Ed also uses the services of Oscar for fix-it jobs around the house and was surprised to find he also delivered water. When I told him the charge was $60 Ed gave me some valuable information for the next time I ordered water. Ed said the Ranch contracts out the water delivery system to several carriers. The contract gives the companies the rights to deliver water to all the homes in the community. The set price for a truckload of water was $45 for all the Ranch houses. Ed just saved me $15 each time I needed a refill of my cistern. He was watching my back. Knowledge is valuable in Mexico.

Chapter 24
Joining in

Yesterday, July 9, marked the first day Suzanne and I were able to participate in a few of the events found on the activities calendar available to all Ranch residents. Due to the lower population staying for the summer months, not all the scheduled games are well attended. The only event during the day having an abundance of residents is the pool volleyball game starting at 12:30 and again in the evenings when the 'all men' or 'all women' games are held. During the evening events and tournaments, the ex-jocks, who probably played some type of sport either in high school or adult leagues, can become serious about winning and loosing. The 12:30 p.m. games are suppose to be a fun time for new and old players.

Suzanne was scheduled to go to town by 1:00 p.m. and help at the ZAPP clinic, which spays and neuters dogs and cats for free. The idea behind such a clinic is to stop the breeding of stray animals. Such dogs and cats are found everywhere in third-world countries, usually in a poor state of health and care. Steve Forman is the man operating the clinic, and volunteers are from all the communities in or around the town of San Felipe. My wife was on the wake-up team helping the animals recover after their operations in the morning. Petting and holding them as the knockout drugs wore off seemed to be her job for the afternoon.

Working for the clinic was the best way for Suzanne to give back to a program that was making a difference in Mexico. Since we started driving down in 2005 a shift has come about. After 2008 we did not see any dead dogs along the road. I heard the spay and neuter clinics were happening in Mexicali as well, and the evidence of such a service appeared to be the lack of stray dogs, alive or dead, seen along highway 5 between Mexicali and San Felipe. I do not know what is happening on the Pacific side of Baja, but I can attest to the lack of a body count found on the roads we traveled from the border to the Ranch.

While Suzanne worked at the ZAPP clinic, I headed to the pool area for the scheduled cribbage game. I arrived around 1:00 p.m. The pool activities director sent me to the Pavilion and said to ask for Sandy, who put on different games for the Ranch residents. I found her with two other women playing a game called San Felipe Rummy, a south of the border version of Gin Rummy. When I asked if I could watch, Sandy instead sat me down in her place and proceeded to coach me as I played the last three hands. For all you residents who know the game, you know the last ones are the most difficult.

My ability to play Gin Rummy allowed my brain to pick up the details of the game quickly and play the next complete round of 12 different hands by myself. Big money is passed between players, with a buy-in of 90 cents. No pesos are allowed and the winner could walk away with a couple of dollars or enough to pay for the soft drink consumed during the afternoon of play. I was able to hold my own but still lost 50 cents by 4:15. The game ended and I needed to hurry into town and pick up Suzanne from the clinic seven miles away. I thanked the women for allowing me to play and learn the game, vowing to return again and sharpen my skills.

All three women were single and living on the Ranch by themselves. During the time I have lived here, I have learned about the population of single women who have outlived husbands and have made El Dorado and the surrounding communities their home. Most live well on their fixed-income in beautiful homes built either with their husbands when they were alive or after they passed. Being only 100 miles from the border and most still driving, the low cost of living allows them to visit family in the States and friends still living north of the border. A few of these women have expressed to me the need of more single older men to come down and try out the lifestyle of Mexico and the community they live in. One woman named Valeria told me the Ranch needs new blood. Most of the single men she has come across are "Brain-dead and just breathing."

I have nothing in the form of evidence to disclaim her comment and I will leave the observation at that. In the defense of the single men living here or even thinking about moving here and looking for an interesting single woman, you better have your 'A game' on. The ladies I played cards with on Saturday were quick on their feet, could carry on a conversation regarding many different subjects and still beat me in San Felipe Rummy. Many are involved in several service groups including the Rotary and Lions Club, Red Cross, ZAPP (organization for spaying and neutering cats and dogs) and still find time to enjoy the many games played on the Ranch and private homes in the area.

During the time it took me to drive to town, Suzanne walked to our favorite restaurant on the malecon or boardwalk by the sea called the Taco Factory. Because it is located right on the ocean, cool breezes usually are blowing onshore. Nature's air-conditioning is doing its job keeping the stores located in this prime real estate location at a lower temperature than businesses only a block away.

When I arrived at the restaurant, Suzanne had been alone for half an hour, drinking a coke and eating her favorite food, guacamole dip with chips. This was also a milestone for my wife. She was finally feeling comfortable enough to walk through town alone, order some food and watch the life of San Felipe going by on the malecon. When we first started coming down to the Ranch in 2005, being alone in town would not have been possible for Suzanne. She is approaching a month of living in Mexico and her comfort level is expanding. She is much more at ease with the population and able to use her few

Spanish vocabulary words to get what she needs. You go, girl.

Adjusting to Mexico: This story is a good tip for the reader thinking of such a move to Mexico, Central America or even South America. Getting to know the population and how they do things is important in adapting to a lifestyle outside your home. When you are in your house, living in a community with Canadians, Americans and Europeans as your neighbors you do not have the noises, population and rhythm of your adopted country right outside your door. Your satellite TV gives you all the news and shows you enjoyed watching back in the States. The computer age we live in connects you with friends via the Internet, Skype or an international telephone call. As one friend of mine told me after living here for thirteen years, "When I am home, I am in America. When I leave my house and the Ranch, I am in Mexico."

I now can understand why populations of immigrants who came to America over the years tended to move to the neighborhoods where others from their home country lived. Not only do the neighbors speak the same language, they also enjoy the same foods, sports interests and engage in the topics of conversations shared by everyone in the streets. China Town, Little Poland and Irish communities are just a few of the many such pockets of immigrant populations found in major cities. The Chinese are probably the most well known group that held onto their language and customs. Where they live in San Francisco, China Town has become one of the most visited tourist destinations in the city by the Bay. Everything from chopsticks to brass dragons can be purchased and the countless restaurants found throughout this section of the city provide the visitor with authentic food from this Asian society.

Food Information: Now that we are living in a community only 100 miles from the border, those members of the Ranch who still hold onto their American diets can make the shopping dash to the border. As I mentioned before, they can purchase food at Wal-Mart, Costco, and Vons and return the same day loaded with all the items for their large pantries, thus enabling them to only shop for fresh vegetables and fruit grown in Mexico. Not all of the community adheres to such a food regimen. After talking to a few of the long-term residents, I discovered their trips to El Centro are limited to only a few times a year. This usually happens when they have a physical with their doctors in the states.

There is one store in the town that is trying to provide the residents from the north with many of the items not available in a Mexican mercado. I have seen products he has purchased in the big box stores in the states with brand names such as Kirkland on the containers. His attempt to provide the large American and Canadian population with the things they want without having to make the two-hours drive to the north seems to be working. His store is expanding and looking more like a grocery store in the States selling everything from cottage cheese to motor oil. The owner is Chinese and his whole family participates in the running of the business. He speaks no English and I believe little Spanish but his children speak Spanish as well as a little English. He and his family are probably the only Chinese nationals living in San Felipe. His attempt to provide the surrounding communities with items only found in California or Arizona, and eliminating the drive north, is just another example of finding a need and filling it.

Smaller stores in our area are also trying to provide the residents with foods from the States. I asked the owner of the Rancho store near El Dorado for the Kashi brand of cereal made by health-minded companies. The owner promised to add it to the list of shopping items. Since Suzanne and I are new and still adjusting to the lifestyle of Mexico in an American community, we will continue to make the run to the border at least once a month. I do not know how often we will travel to the States a year from now but I do know the adjustment is gradual, and the longer we are here the easier things become. We will head to El Centro and Brawley on Friday for an initial doctor's visit after transferring our medical records from the Phoenix area.

Mexico is making an attempt to copy some of the favorite items becoming popular in the American diet. An example of an item produced in Mexico is soymilk. The soymilk made in the States cost 40 pesos. The same size soymilk container with Spanish written on the carton cost 21 pesos or almost half the cost of the one made 100 miles to the north. Hain is the company making the Mexican soymilk and Kirkland has also added a Mexican brand for their Costco stores. Because so many Americans are changing their diet, especially in their golden years, the product line of health foods has grown. The consumer has a choice to make. He can purchase the made-in-America product or the Mexican product for half the price. I have tried the soymilk 'hecho en Mexico' and the only difference is that the local product is a little thicker.

The further one lives from the border, the more cost of American products goes up. The cost of transportation with high gas prices plus demand can make a box of cereal made by Kashi increase from $3.50 to $5.00 easily. As more North Americans continue to retire in communities in Mexico and the desired food items making up their diet in the States are requested, word will get out to Mexican companies to produce their version of the same product at a lower price. Mexicans may or may not make the change for healthy food in their own diet but Americans will because they want items they are familiar with.

In American stores such as Von's there is a section called Hispanic foods, which caters to the population eating those items. In the future stores in cities throughout Mexico may have sections called Yankee or Gringo foods providing the items non-Hispanics eat. 'Back at ya Americanos'.

Mail

I have also given this topic a special heading because contact with home is very important for the North Americans. Here is how the mail reaches many communities south of the border, and so far it has been working. A courier service travels each day to the little town of Calexico, across the border from Mexicali. Letters and packages arrive at the same P.O. box in Calexico and are transported south to the different drop off stations in the San Felipe area. We have a mail service in a small strip mall next to the Ranch and I have seen one in town for those Yankees who either live in the developments to the south or in the town itself. One more town, Puertecitos, lays 50 miles south of San Felipe and I believe the mail service goes to that town as well, bringing news and information from home.

A quick note regarding other communities in Mexico is this: Any person who wants to move to a town south of the border needs to check out how mail reaches them. This is important if you are still dependent upon paper mail for information. The computer age is changing the need for mail service each year. If mail is still necessary do your research before moving.

A note about the communities south of San Felipe may be of some interest to the reader. Along the coastline south of San Felipe, many solar homes were built twenty or thirty years ago. The population I was told started with hippies from the 60's and 70's who may have moved to the area to escape the draft, the

Vietnam War, or they may be marijuana smugglers who retired and may not be able to return to the States because their pictures appeared at one time on a U.S. post office wall. The inhabitants are unique types of Americans who have spent much of their lives south of the border, and the rugged living seems to have chiseled deep lifelines into their faces, giving some residents the unique features similar to Keith Richards of the Rolling Stones.

There are a few decent homes in the community of Puertecitos. Other than the cove beach in the center of town, and a shack the size of an outhouse used as a lending library for the readers inhabiting the town, not much else stands out. The hot springs were mentioned earlier in the book and continue to bring scalding water down to the Sea of Cortez to be mixed with the seawater in a unique hot-tub experience.

Post Office and Library in Puertecitos

Banking

Yesterday marked one month and four days of calling the Ranch and San Felipe my home. The week before we purchased a local phone, so we were now able to complete the banking application with a phone number in case they needed to call us. The weeks before getting a phone I simply removed dollars from my bank in the states and changed the currency at the border crossing, looking for the red flashing signs indicating the purchase rate for pesos and dollars. When I first started coming to Mexico in 2005 the exchange rate hovered around 10 pesos for each dollar traded. When the economy started to falter right before the 2008 election the exchange rate started to climb and at one time the rate jumped to more than thirteen pesos for a dollar. Today, July 12, the exchange rate hovers between 10.80 peso and 11.50 pesos depending upon where you are. Near the border the exchange rate is higher than in San Felipe a hundred miles south. The moneychanger's rate is not the best in Mexico. One needs a peso account from a bank for the higher exchange.

FM Information: Getting a Peso account is important for residents who are living here in Mexico and plan on obtaining their FM-2 or FM-3 residence papers. The FM papers are for a person staying in Mexico and planning on living here full time. These papers are also important in letting the government keep tab of your intentions as to how long you plan to stay and live in Mexico. We have an FM-1, which used to be called a tourist visa and is good for six months. Our 'go to' guy, Ed, said there is little need for us to apply for the more expensive FM-2 and FM-3 papers He suggested to Suzanne and myself, since we were only going to rent and not build right away, to get the tourist or FM-1 visa and keep renewing it every six months. The tourist visa cost 25 dollars for six months. The other visas cost hundreds of dollars and holding off such costs as long as possible is the better way to function when first moving to Mexico. Since the laws do change in Mexico, it is best to go to the office in your community that deals with the immigration paperwork and see which set of documents you need depending upon your situation.

(Update 2013) As of this year a new FM law has been passed. Homeowners purchase either a temporary or permanent residence visa. Depending upon how long a time period you purchase determines the cost of the visa. This is a new law and subject to change at any time. Stay tuned. Check with the immigration office in San Felipe for the latest update.

Bancomer or BBVA was the bank other residents told us to go to. The affiliate bank in the states is Compass Bank. Both banks may be under the same banner as far as ownership, but having an account in the States with Compass Bank does not give you the same privileges one receives with a Bancomer account in Mexico. The directions given to us by other residents when opening an account are as follows. As you enter the bank see a woman by the name of Gabby, in the first office stall to the left. Three weeks before I made the trip to get the paperwork in order to open an account I met Gabby. She handles all the Canadian and American clients with their accounts. During the period of obtaining the paper work and actually opening a peso account, Suzanne and I obtained the needed phone numbers and addresses of three friends we knew on the Ranch who would vouch for us. We chose two people we had rented houses from in the past six years and Henry, our rental manager, who we have known for a few years.

Gabby is an educated mother of three children, who transferred to San Felipe from Rocky Point a year ago. She already had a big fan base with many of the other clients. Her helpful manner and patience with the Americans having to fill out the paperwork became a useful asset. In our conversation with her, we learned of a town called San Carlos on the mainland. She was from northern Mexico and she promised to be our personal travel agent when we started to explore Mexico in the fall and winter. This is when the temperatures start to drop and travel in this warm southern country becomes much more comfortable.

"I know a lot about the northern part of Mexico because I was born there," Gabby said in her perfect American English.

When I asked her if she had lived in the States she answered, "No, I just watch a lot of American programs on TV and I picked up the accent by listening to the shows."

Wanting to find out more about her as we were signing all the papers that come with opening an account in Mexico, she told us she lived a boring life. Having three children ages 6, 4 and 2 did not allow much free time other than work and home with the kids. Her children must be learning English as well if their mother watches American programs all the time. Speaking English as a second language is very helpful in obtaining work in Mexico, and usually the pay is higher for those who are bi-lingual.

(Update 2013) Gabby has moved on to another job on the mainland of Mexico and her sister, Josephina, has taken over her job. She is just as cute as Gabby and her English is very good as well.

The peso account needs $300 to be opened and if such a balance is maintained. there are no service charges. Mexico prefers that gringos deposit checks instead of cash when transferring monies from the States. That way the fear of money being laundered is eliminated. A few hundred dollars placed into the account does not present a problem. Being in Mexico was starting to feel like the Wild West, with so many restrictions placed on banking.

At the same time, Mexico was trying to do their part in the war on drugs. The only drawback to having a check deposited has to do with the time it takes to clear. Twelve working days is the waiting period after making a deposite, and this temporary wait period lasts for three months. After the three months, the time limit drops to seven working days. Such time limits are done to enable banks to clear the checks and hold onto the money. Banks collect interest, or lend it out to others at a high interest rate. They make money on currency in all the different accounts. Banks are not stupid and this is why they have the nicest buildings in every town in America as well as in Mexico.

We finished our business with Gabby and headed to DJ's Mercado in town to pick up a few items not found in the small markets near the Ranch. For the next two days we filled our social calendars with events. Learning to play Mexican dominoes and the weekly social visit to a resident's house including a tour, finger food and conversation with others living on the Ranch completed the social week.

Mexican Dominoes

July 13 found us at the beautiful home of a woman named Cathy Lee whom we met at a social function at our neighbor's house. Several residents like to take the newbie under their wing and get them involved with the social connections of the Ranch. This was evident with Cathy Lee bending over backward to set up a learning session at her house for the game of Mexican dominoes.

Cathy Lee was also able to get Suzanne into a book club, which started in the fall by asking a member who did not seem to be all that interested in books. The member was ready to let her membership go and Suzanne took her place. Books for Suzanne are a big part of her life and she reads around 20 books to my 1. Suzanne, raised by her single mother for many years, enjoyed a trip to the library as the family's source of entertainment while growing up. Her mother, Alice, also read every night, and for the last few years of her life Suzanne kept quite busy keeping her mother stocked in literature.

Finding a person's home on the Ranch where we live can be quite exciting and almost an adventure. The hillside homes are accessed through different gated entrances with guards checking everyone's car through. Each resident has a sticker on their automobile showing they belong on the Ranch. The guard at the gate opens the blockade for the driver when the Ranch decal is seen. The non-resident service people bringing water and gas to a house are documented when they enter. They are also documented when they leave and where they went.

After entering the correct gate the road signs direct the driver to the different development sites including such exotic names as Buena Vista or good view, Hacienda del Sol or home of the sun (very appropriate name in the summer), and Playa del Mar or beach of the ocean. After finding the correct turn off, the person giving directions usually points out different landmarks one may find on the drive to their house, or mention the street names. Our house is just off of Solar Ave. in an area with electricity. Many homes do not have street names so a block sign number must be found and after that a lot number. Now that so many homes have been built and the different colors and shapes adorn the landscape, directions may be given like this:

"Turn right by the white house with the huge Palapa in the back. Drive towards the red mountain until you see two new houses being built on the right. Turn to the left and we are the salmon-colored home with the fountain in the front patio. Park and come in."

We found Cathy Lee's home without much problem. Two other new players arrived at the same time so we knew we had found the correct house. Most of the social events on the Ranch or in any American community in Mexico involve food. Snack food is the usual offering at most events and the variety can extent from the simple such as popcorn to the extreme like shrimp sushi. The latter goes quickly so unless you want to snack on popcorn at a social event, don't be shy getting in the food line right away.

After the introductions between the players, we all sat at the table with a pile of dominoes spread out facing down. A centerpiece in the middle acted as a train station and little plastic trains of different colors adorned each place around the train station. Each player had one of the different colored trains. Many of the seasoned players bring their own markers to the weekly events, such as jeweled studded geckos or other representatives of the Mexican desert. Players on the Ranch pick up markers in their travels to other towns and cities throughout Baja or mainland Mexico. The dominoes are color coded to make the identification of each number ranging from 0 to 12 easier than trying to count the dots on each individual piece.

After a few sessions of play, in which Suzanne won the first two rounds, the main strategies of the game became clear. For the next few hours, with breaks in-between for the smokers, we began our orientation into one of the most popular pastimes on the Ranch and maybe other communities throughout Mexico. The warm summers dictate how one is to spend the months of July through September. Indoor activities are the best way to pass the time, visit other homes and learn about the latest news on the Ranch. Water volleyball players may argue with this statement but not everyone can participate in that sport.

The game ended when one of the couples needed to return to their home to start the generator in order to cool off their house for the evening. Suzanne and I remained for another hour talking about telephones, health insurance and other topics affecting our lives in Mexico. As I have mentioned before, most owners are willing to pass on what they know about each subject, and the magnitude of all the different answers can overwhelm any new resident. We were no different. We went home, ate dinner and soon found our way to the bedroom. Suzanne woke around 2:30 the next morning with all the information she had heard the previous day floating around in her head. She could not sleep. When something like this happens a nap the next day is appropriate.

One Day at a Time: A note to any new resident of Mexico or third-world country is this: Take each challenge one at a time and ask how others are having their needs met. The answers will vary, and finding the best answer for you is all you have to do. When being overwhelmed starts to set in, step back from the problem. You do not have to have an answer all at once.

Many of you reading this book may be retired. If no one can phone you for a few days or you cannot access your e-mail until Friday there is still no problem. The world of instant answers does not pertain to you any more. The solutions will come and things will get figured out. Take a breath and know you are living a unique life. With the different living experience come different hurdles. Problems arise and are solved. You will be fine in the meantime.

Chapter 25
Steve Forman

"Can you tell your wife Steve died yesterday?" asked Suzanne, our neighbor, as she drove up to our house the next morning.

"Steve?" I asked.

"The man whose clinic she worked at on Saturday."

That's how I found out about the death of Steve Forman. My neighbor heard the news and in this small community any news travels quickly. He was the man who kept the ZAPP clinic going in town for the free spaying and neutering of cats and dogs in the area. Suzanne had spent her previous Saturday helping the animals awake after their surgeries.

The story I heard was Steve had driven to El Centro and suffered a heart attack while in his car in a parking lot. The news sent a shock wave throughout the community. This was a man who dedicated his life to keeping the clinic running, and is part of the reason you do not see stray dogs and cats around the town of San Felipe. He was responsible for having many fundraising events in the area, including the Friday before

Memorial Day party at Playa de Oro, which I happened to attend after bringing my second load of household items into Mexico. Also the Diva Show from San Diego, which comes down to San Felipe several times each year, is a fundraiser for the clinic. Both Suzanne and I attended the Diva Show with our neighbors, everyone still on the Ranch and surrounding communities. It was a huge turnout.

According to my neighbor, Steve really made an impact on the community and the little Mexican town of San Felipe. His good works will not be forgotten. Many of the residents have a dog or cat from the clinic or through Steve, who was dedicated to finding homes for all the animals he came into contact with. I think the community is waiting for someone who will step up and take Steve's place and carry on his work.

I am mentioning Steve because of the impact he made. There are situations in Mexico and other third-world countries needing help in order to change. Living in Mexico allows those experiencing the culture to see ways they can give back to their adopted country and feel good about the impact they make. Steve did his part and will be remembered by everyone who knew him and were impacted by his love for animals.

Steve Forman at his Memorial Day fund-raiser for ZAPP, 2011

Chapter 26
Return Trip to California

The day after finding out about Steve Forman, Suzanne and I needed to return to the medical clinic in Brawley. Returning to the States and visiting the communities of Calexico, El Centro and Brawley are similar to border communities along other states such as Arizona and Texas. The primary language is Spanish and the need for almost any job held in the towns is the ability to converse in both English and Spanish. Many workers I came across in the big box stores such as Wal-Mart and Vons spoke Spanish to each other and English to the non-Hispanic shoppers who came in. Even the bank employees at Chase where capable of speaking English and Spanish, while Spanish remained the first language to 90% of the customers entering and making a deposit or withdrawal. This area is truly a bi-lingual region of America.

The first stop for us was at the brand-new shopping mall just outside El Centro off highway 8. In our search for the AT&T store to get phones with the Mexico plan we discovered a large theater complex. The times for the showing of the last Harry Potter film were noted. Later on the evening news we heard the film set sales records around the world for a first day showing. It knocked off the second of The Twilight Series vampire movies by 20 million dollars and will probably break the all time record of whatever film holds that honor at the moment. We decided to try and get all our errands completed and return by 6:30 to add our dollars to the record being set.

AT&T was located near the theater and, because the complex was so new, few customers were in the store. Usually phone stores are swamped with shoppers looking for the newest gadget or phone to keep them in the loop with all their friends. A young lady assisted us for an hour and a half helping us choose two simple phones. We signed up for the Mexican plan and transferred all our information from the Verizon phones into the address book of the new phones.

As we walked out of the store I saw a look of relief in the eyes of Suzanne. She now held a device that would enable her to keep in contact with her friends in the U.S. and me if she was visiting in the States and needed to call. AT&T is the only reliable phone company with the "Call Mexico" plan at this time. I am amazed how Carlos Slim, the Mexican owner of Telcel, was able to sell the service to AT&T and simply let go of the headache of servicing the customers and collect a check from the American company each month. Genius.

We were now connected with the States through television, phones and Internet. I still had to use the Wi-Fi through the Ranch either at the pool, Ranch office or Pavilion. Our neighbors are willing to let us piggyback onto their satellite system, but we are still waiting. We need a booster system, to enable the signal to pass through the thick walls of our house. I can pick up their signal when I position a chair in front of our garage and aim the computer at my neighbor's window. I can then read my e-mail.

Our plan is to try a booster first so we can do any computer network duties from within the house, away from the heat of the summer and the cool of the winter.

Our doctor's appointment was not until 3:30. We made one more stop at the post office and found Starbucks for a Suzanne fix. We checked into another hotel offering good rates for Ranch visitors in El Centro. A quick nap was in order and then off to Clinicas de Salud Del Pueblo, Inc. I kept seeing the word salud everywhere when driving to Brawley, and wondered how salad was mixed in with all the names of medical buildings. After looking up the word it made sense. Health and salad go together so that is how I remember the Spanish word for health.

Suzanne and I do not believe we found the clinic our neighbors told us about. They said there was a good one in Brawley but without specific directions, we were at the mercy of the population of Brawley. We filled out the intake forms at home during the two weeks since our last visit. Suzanne, our neighbor, must have gone to another clinic, which we still have not seen or visited. I knew right away we probably were at a different one based on the forms we filled out at home.

Are you homeless?   Y (SI) N
Are you addicted to drugs?   Y (SI) N
Are you employed?   Y (SI) N
Do you have any mental problems? Y (SI) N

This was a clinic serving anyone who needed help. Here is the best statement I can make regarding this clinic: Everyone working there was the friendliest staff I have ever experienced. Both Suzanne and I were treated better than in any other medical facility in California or Arizona. We felt we were guided here, and we decided to not try and find the clinic other Ranch residents used.

The waiting room at 3:30 in the afternoon was filled with a population of Spanish-speaking residents. We were the only non-Hispanic people in the building. Having lived in Flagstaff for ten years, I shopped in Wal-Mart on Saturdays and know what it feels like to be a minority. In Flagstaff, the Navajo and Hopi population take over the store in numbers. They buy enough supplies for their homes back on the reservation. In Brawley the town and all the neighboring communities are Hispanic, so this was not a weekend experience. This is what the population is.

The reader needs to remember this historical fact. When the U.S. took Texas, Arizona and California from Mexico, they did not ship the Mexican population back across the border and have them sign up for citizenship. They were instant Americans because they lived in these areas before and they continue to live in these towns and communities today.

Suzanne and I were called within a few minutes to proceed to our different medical practitioner while others in the waiting rooms remained. I found out later many people waiting were drop-in patients and they needed to wait until those who have an appointment are served. By 5 p.m. Suzanne and I were both seen by our medical practitioners and checked out. Suzanne needed a few tests done and had to return in the morning to have blood drawn. I was given an EKG and also set up to see a chiropractor in two weeks. I also received the name of an acupuncturist in town. I used the needle-in-the-skin approach to treat numbness in my legs while living in Phoenix and found the procedure a much better solution than taking another drug.

My practitioner was attentive and listened to my stories of living in Mexico and my project of writing a book about making the transition south of the border. I told her my visit today would probably make it into a chapter because I was at the point of documenting the move on a day-to-day basis. She and her husband, who worked for the border patrol in some capacity, had good jobs. She told me she worked at different clinics in the area. She agreed with me that the clinic we had chosen did have a friendly staff, which made her work easier. Before leaving she prescribed nitroglycerin and said I needed to carry it with me at all times. Because I had a heart attack in 2002 and a stint was put in, I remained at risk. The nitro would be helpful in case of a return heart problem. Also I now lived over 100 miles from the States, and the nitro could save me in case of an emergency.

A trip to Wal-Mart on the outskirts of Brawley to purchase medications, shopping for a few items not found in San Felipe, and dinner at an authentic Mexican restaurant just up the road completed our day. We were tired and Harry Potter would have to wait. We returned to the hotel located in El Centro just across from Starbucks. After a shower we were asleep by 9. The day was successful. Communication from Mexico to the States had been purchased through AT&T. Prescriptions were filled and banking needs completed in one day. I even got a haircut in the Hispanic barbershop across from the clinic the next morning while Suzanne was having blood drawn.

Suzanne was dropped off at Greyhound the next morning to catch the bus to San Diego while still eating her breakfast burrito. We said our good-bys. I would not be back up until June 28 and she would be with her niece in Ramona, CA during this period. The trip was planned months before because one of Roxie's horses was going to have a foal and Suzanne wanted to be there when it happened.

My last stop was to pick up a few items in a box store like Vons or Albertsons in Calexico because I did not want to backtrack into El Centro after dropping off Suzanne at Greyhound. No such luck. Food for Less and another Wal-Mart make up the food possibilities in this growing community. I chose Wal-Mart because I knew they carried Kashi cereals. This is an organic brand of a healthy breakfast choice. When I parked in the lot I discovered where all the cars with Baja license plates coming from Mexico went. Three quarters of all the autos in the lot had Baja plates, and the store was like being in a Wal-Mart in Mexico. Spanish was the first language spoken, and by now one would think I would know this fact. I do now. Many of the Mexican residents came across the border to purchase items not available in the Mexicali stores.

Money Exchange: The drive back to San Felipe produced the routine stops at the money exchangers and the gas station. Another note to the reader wanting to live in Mexico is this: After you have opened your Peso account with Bancomer or any other Mexican bank, take any cash in dollars to that bank to exchange for pesos. The best rate at the money exchangers before and after the border was 11.35 pesos for the dollar. My new bank exchanged the dollar at the daily rate of 11.60 pesos. This was 25 centavos per dollar more than the rate on the streets. When multiplied by $100 the difference is 25 pesos or 250 pesos per $1000 or 2500 peso for $10,000. It does add up, so remember this when exchanging money.

(2014 update.) This is a money exchange tip for those of you who buy this book. A few of the gas stations in San Felipe and the one near the Ranch post an exchange rate for pesos and dollars. Most people think this is a ploy by the stations to get the driver to use their station and get the best exchange rate when buying gas. The rate is better than that offered by the banks. If the boss is not around the attendants will exchange your dollars at the high rate posted outside the station. Do not get greedy. $20 or $40 at a time is best. I use them instead of driving all the way into town and changing cash at the bank. (This is Mexico so the practice may change at any time. This is my disclaimer just in case the banks get mad and stop this money exchange from happening.)

Customer Service: Here is another piece of information for the reader who is contemplating a move to another country: When you have a good experience with a service provider such as a gas station, bank or medical clinic, then continue using that business. Not only will they get to know you but also you will get to know them. They will continue giving the best service to a return customer. There are many gas stations throughout Mexico. The residents where I live usually have their favorites, especially when they travel to the border and want to fill up just before crossing into California. Gas in the States can be 50 to 75 cents a gallon more. Find out from friends the one they use and see if your experience is as good as theirs. Support the good people that give good service and they will stay in business. Tip well and maintain your best attitude possible.

Remember; each of us in Mexico is an ambassador representing our perspective countries. If you leave a poor impression at a business, the next American may have to pay the price for your behavior by receiving poor service and so on. There is a commercial that used to air on TV showing good acts, by people who are observed by others, who in turn do good acts who are observed by others, and so on. This is an important truth for those living in foreign countries. You are being watched all the time, so be your best and it will come back to you in many good ways.

Chapter 27
When Suzanne is Away… I Will Play

Now that the house is in order and all the major obstacles have been removed from our 'To Do' list, a routine is a good thing to create. Life in Mexico or any other Latin American country is never going to be the same as the town or city from where you may have moved. The year Suzanne and I spent in Peoria, Arizona after living in Flagstaff, Arizona for ten years was an eye opener to life in a city. We rented a condo in a retirement community.

The Phoenix area has many such developments. A small community pool was a short walk away, and a short drive from Union Hills to Bell Road put us within reach of banks, restaurants, mall stores and a post office. There was even a major league ballpark used for the Spring Training camps of the San Diego Padres and Seattle Mariners. A massage center, gas station and Midas service center were in walking distance from the complex where we lived. While living in the community for a year, both our neighbors had to retire to assisted living due to health issues. The area was great but the older population needing more care was a challenge. I guess they reminded us of what we may be facing in ten to twenty years.

Starbucks was also within walking distance and Suzanne's addiction to good coffee could be met easily. Olive Garden, The Pita Jungle, The Elephant Bar, P.F. Chang and countless Mexican restaurants rounded out the culinary eating establishments built to satisfy the needs and desires of any taste bud. Stores to fix your computer and sell countless additions to your electronic world could be found along with the latest flat screen TVs at Best Buy. I believe the statement, "If they don't have it you don't need it", is true for the location where we lived. Making a complete transition from all these sensory delights and moving to a community in Mexico can be a shock to your system and you may suffer from stimulation with-drawl. Even the most modern communities in Mexico will not have the same the level of services available in the States.

General Observation: Most of the long-time residents I have met on the Ranch do not need to return to the States as often as the new residents. Ed Jones says he only goes to the States once or twice a year. He probably combines medical trips with purchasing the latest electronic gadget for his increasing computer needs, and maybe picks up a few food items for his pantry. I heard he just returned from El Centro and became sick. He probably drank the water in California. Because his body was used to the water in Mexico, the different organisms found in the California water could have knocked him around a bit. The same thing happens when tourists come to Mexico and pick up the Mexican variety of microbes in the water or food.

Now that I have documented the different stimulations available in the States, I will try to describe how the locals cope and fill their day in the summer with other activities where we live.

Yesterday was Monday and Bunko is the name of the game. With only a handful of residents on the Ranch, the Bunko match was played in the air-conditioned activities trailer with two tables and four players at each table (mesa). An activities employee and I were the only male participants in the game. Two dollars or twenty pesos completed the buy-in. The goal was to complete four rounds and then split up the pot into several categories. The most Bunko wins, the last Bunko win, and the most losses made up the prize categories.

My first day with Bunko did not help my new standings among the regular players who made the Monday event a part of their lives. I won the first six games without a loss and had one Bunko as well. I remained in my lucky seat for most of the afternoon and managed to end up winning two of three awards available for the game. I left with 100 pesos in my pocket, or around $10. I will return next week so the ladies can have a chance to win some of their money back. The players have decided to up the ante to $4 or 40 pesos for the buy-in. If I do as well as yesterday, the women may move the game to a different location and forget to tell me where it is.

The games at 1:00 P.M. provide the residents with a chance to get out of the house and turn off the AC. Staying cool under the Ranch's air conditioner and visiting with each other to find out the latest news is important. Each day presents a new type of entertainment. Today I plan to attend the Mexican Dominoes event, a game I learned last week. The pool is nearby, so after the games are completed, a dip and relaxing by the water offers a great way to round off the afternoon during the hot, humid summer in the Baja. Any duties around the house can be completed in the morning unless you swim laps or do water aerobics at that time.

San Felipe Rummy is a favorite and played on Wednesdays

July 20, 2011 and the warm weather continues. The humidity on the Sea of Cortez seems to come and go. When the weather contains moisture in the air, I wake up and my arms are sticking to other parts of my body. I now have an indication as to what to wear for the day. Clothes you do not want to have sweat stains on are left in the closet and the 'I do not care what you do to me' clothes are brought out. In my wardrobe this usually means a tee shirt and shorts. From this combination the mix and match choices are endless. I usually hold onto tee shirts for a long time, and if they are made from 100% cotton, like the ones I purchased in Peru in 2006, they are still in my collection.

Arriving at Juanito's Cantina, located across from the swimming pool on the Ranch, I entered a room filled with players sitting at three tables. They were poised as though they were about to play high-stakes poker. They did not want any distractions getting in their way. The entertainment schedule starts all the games at 1:00 P.M. I was told by a few of the women from the Bunko game the serious players arrive a half-hour early in order to secure a seat and not be left watching the game from the sidelines. This was the position I was in at the moment. Several of the tables only play with certain other players, so seats are saved for them. A new arrival held little chance of sitting at the reserved tables. Wanting to meet new people was not a high priority on their list.

Five minutes before 1:00 p.m. three more women arrived and with one of the activities directors, a fourth table of five players was put together just as the clock was ticking down. The start time had a ritual feeling to it and many of the players counted off the last seconds, giving the game a more serious edge than the easy-flowing Bunko game from the previous afternoon.

Like all the games, there is a small buy-in fee. The players pay $3 or 30 pesos and, instead of winning cash, Ranch coupons worth a dollar each are given to the winners of the games. This tactic gets around the 'no gambling' laws of the area. Had the Ranch been built in the States on a reservation, a five-star casino would have been erected by now with the winners paid in cash and not Ranch Bucks.

Our table started playing after the countdown finished. Even though we had one less player than the other tables, we finished fifteen minutes later due to a smoke break by two of our players. While sitting at the table, I was again seated next to Fran and across from her friend Valera. They had taught me the game of San Felipe Rummy a few weeks before. Fran was in her 80's and she was one of the sharpest of any woman on the Ranch. I wanted to ask her more about her life.

As I mentioned before, I found a large population of women existed who had either outlived their husbands or were single and had moved to the development on their own. Fran has lived on the Ranch for over 20 years. She continued to stay after her husband of 55 years passed on. She said she had no desire to return to the States. She felt safer living in Baja on the Ranch instead of another such community located either in Arizona or another retirement state. Her limited retirement income went further in Mexico and she had the funds to travel if she wanted to visit relatives north of the border.

Valera, who found out about the Ranch development while living in Berkley, California, also shared the same feelings of safety and contentment living in Baja. She was a retired opera singer with a sharp mind and sought out individuals who were interesting to talk to. She was the resident who coined the term 'brain-dead and breathing' while describing many of the single men living in the area. Any man wanting to get to know her needed to be able to think on his feet and express himself in greater depth than any regulars hanging out at any sports bars on or near the Ranch. I found out there is even a support group made up of this population of single women who live their life in Baja.

Suzanne is still in Ramona, and I received an e-mail from her after playing dominoes while doing laundry near Playa de Oro. Her heart rate was high. She was able to fix the problem by filling a prescription at the CVC pharmacy. She also ate some mushrooms in a lasagna dish served at her niece's party celebrating one of her Arabian horses having a filly. Suzanne is allergic to mushrooms, and all she could do was sleep and allow the effects from the fungus to pass through her body. AT&T allowed me to give her a quick call and receive assurance she would be fine. The 'ET call home' plan worked.

As I walked into the laundry near Playa de Oro I met a woman and her desert dog. She had been there since 10:00 A.M. and it was now 4 P.M. She started to share her day with me, not caring whether I was interested or not. After loading ten washers with a few weeks of laundry, she discovered the quarter machine was empty. She had only enough coins for washing the ten loads she planned to do that day. Not enough coins to dry them. Thirty minutes after she arrived. the power in the complex was turned off and remained so for the next hour and a half. Lack of power shut down the AC in the laundry room and automatically locked the doors of the building. The locked doors meant she and the regular laundry woman who irons and washes clothes for the local residents were trapped. Her dog was in the car at the time and with his long fur coat he must have been quite hot for the duration of being car bound. Eventually the power returned but she was not able to continue her washday until late in the afternoon.

The woman lived in one of the solar communities along the Sea of Cortez south of San Felipe. She moved there while in her 30's and called San Felipe her home for the past 20 years. She was the type of woman you did not mess with and her toughness was expressed in her dislike for the American government. Her Libertarian views seemed to fit those calling them selves expatriates. She survived for the past two decades doing odd jobs and caring for others in her neighborhood who needed their plants watered or houses cleaned. Her size and desert-like appearance, with the lines on her face deepened by the dry and hot climate of 20 seasons, reminded me of Annie Oakley. She was a part of the movement into Baja before the developers arrived building gated communities, luxury homes and a lifestyle more suitable for many of the inhabitants of the Ranch.

Our conversation eventually spread into worldviews and ways to fix America. I usually find a way to introduce the fact that I am writing a book about my move to Mexico, and I include the title of my first book just to show I might be a credible writer with something to say. She was interested in the nine-year travel book and said she would download it when she got home. The electronic book world is big in Baja. Barnes and Noble and other such bookstores have not made a move into the Mexican communities and do not need to because of the Kindle and Nook devices allowing access to the world of literature.

When my new 'Baja Mama' friend finally finished washing her clothes she packed up the damp items. She was out of quarters to dry them. She called her dog and headed back to her beachfront property south of San Felipe. She and her other neighbors only had fans to keep themselves cool and survive the hot summer, which was now upon us. She owned a clothesline and would use the natural drying method to finish the job when she got home. I have not visited any of the communities south of San Felipe but if I ever did and this woman gave me the tour, I know I would be safe.

Within half an hour my clothes were dry and I too headed back to the rented home we have now turned into a comfortable shelter from the hot, dry breezes of summer in Baja. My evening routine usually included unpacking the car and turning on the AC in the living room. A quick shower helped to remove the summer residue caked on me from either sweat or dust. After a wash, I found my place on the couch with 300 channels to choose from via Direct TV. When Suzanne was home she would perform the same ritual, with the addition of rubbing in lotions and creams. The products promised replenishment of the skin and a return to the youthful look of your 20's, thus keeping the cosmetic world a multi-billion dollar industry based on this vision alone.

House Building: A note to the reader regarding building houses in Mexico. There are several types of build materials. The bottom of the material list is the simple Mexican brick called 'shit brick'. It is called this because it is made using chicken shit in the firing. The top material is a foam cement mixture with a high R factor and insulation from the heat of summer and cold of winter. Windows should be double-paned and a good set of blinds are needed in summer months as the sun passes from the east side of your house to the west. The late afternoons seem to bring the most heat. Many residents have installed large shades for the outside of the house, which drop down over the openings to the porches facing west. This establishes another barrier to the intense afternoon temperatures beating down on the homes found on the Ranch.

I may have repeated several of these tips, but I want to make sure the reader remembers these valuable pieces of information. Knowledge is necessary regarding the cooling of a house in Mexico.

The color of the house is also of importance. The lighter colors, such as a white, tan or cream, appear to be a popular choice with the best ability to reflect the rays of the sun and the high temperatures accompanying those rays. The house Suzanne and I are renting contains none of the mentioned conditions for having a well insulated home. We are faced with the dilemma of protecting ourselves from the hot summer and not have an electric AC bill as high as the monthly rent.

The house is spacious, with many windows surrounding the building, allowing views of the mountains and ocean from any angle. Most of the single-paned windows face the west so the intense heat pours into the dwelling like a magnifying glass trying to light a campfire at a Boy Scout retreat.

Mexican brick and the dark desert-orange color of our home added little to the R factor of protection. In the Sonora Desert the darker colors cause the temperatures in the house to rise rapidly and any cool air from the AC looses its affect if an inhabitant strays further than ten feet from the unit on the wall. The one redeeming factor in the house is the fact it contains AC splits. There is a separate cooling unit for each room. If a space is not being used, then the door is shut to the unused part of the house and the cool air flows only where the person inside the house happens to be. The kitchen/dining room and living room each have a large unit. The two bedrooms have their own smaller units for nighttime deployment, making it possible to sleep in the summer.

Our first line of defense from the heat was to buy material to make curtains for the windows and follow the routine of covering and closing them in the afternoon from 2:00 p.m. on. This is a must. Much of the morning is spent on the porch facing the west where I have shade and occasional breezes coming in from the desert interior. Suzanne has usually finished her sunrise walk by 6:30 or 7 A.M. She retreats into the bedroom on the east side of the house where the fan is the only source of cooling needed since the room is still temperate from the AC running through the night. After I finish my set goal of how many words I want to type and have closed down my front porch operation, I also retreat into the house for meditation and back-stretching yoga. Breakfast and my twenty minutes of audio lessons in Spanish is next. Hopefully the daily practice will translate into my ability to communicate my basic needs to the local population in the future.

By now it is between 9 and 10 a.m. and the plan for the day is mapped out. In the summer it is best to plan for one major event such as banking in town or food shopping. Too many chores will lead to over-exposure to the elements and the possibility of missing one of the calendar events starting at 12:30 and going until 3:00 or 4:00 p.m.

Home by 5:00 with the living room AC blasting in cool air gives us the zone of relief needed to sit and enjoy Jeopardy and Wheel of Fortune, both programs helping to stimulate our sixty-year old minds. An evening show involving some type of police work ranging from Hawaii Five-0 to NCIS rounds out our entertainment.

Suzanne retreats to the bedroom and continues her ritual of reading a chapter or two of a novel she has, either on the Kindle I bought for her or a book from the unread pile. These books are found in one of the three bookcases filled with her personal library. Top authors of our time or the classics which she does not want to let go of complete her library. I make my bedroom appearance and go straight to the pillow. My morning hours are best for my creative side to be expressed and this includes reading. *Breakfast With Buddha* is my current literary endeavor.

I played two new games on Thursday and Friday of this week. My neighbor, Suzanne, needed a fourth in bridge. The last time I played was in Germany in 1970, but I continued to play the hands in the bridge column of the newspaper over the years to keep in practice. I was given a condensed version of a bridge-bidding book being used by the group. Different scenarios are presented to the reader in the form of: "What would you do if your partner bid one no-trump and you had 6 to 8 points in your hand with 5 cards in a major suit?"

Remembering Blackwood, a bidding system used by my college bridge partners, helped a bit, but this cheat sheet had three different conventions to choose from.

The game was held in one of the beautiful condos located near the golf course with a short walk to the Sea of Cortez. The apartment belonged to another single woman, Nikki, who lived full time on the Ranch and built her life in the community of other retired residents. She was a nurse and lived in Japan during the years I spent traveling the world in the 70's. Many of the single women have outlived their spouses and have adjusted to the life in Mexico, living well on their fixed-incomes. Nikki, like many other beautiful, older single women, loves her life in Mexico, and I am sure her having lived in Japan helped her to make the lifestyle transition.

Just a note to you single older men who may think they can come down here to Mexico and sweep these beautiful single women off their feet. These ladies 'got game.' They have life experiences and can tell when someone may be playing them. They also do not necessarily need a man in their life because they are independent and can function well on their own. If you do come down and try to meet some of these women, you better lead with your heart and not looking for, as my friend Cathy Lee says, a 'nurse or a purse'.

The game proceeded with my remembering how to play the bridge hands better than my making the correct bid. Bidding is where I communicate to my partner the best information I can to complete a contract and win the game. The mistakes we made were discussed along with plays made by the other three players. The session became a learning time as well as a pleasant way to pass the 108-degree afternoon in a beautiful condo filled with decorations and items collected by the hostess on her world travels. Nikki ended up as the winner, with a victory with each of us as her partner. My only win, with the hostess, fired up my desire to play again when asked to fill in for a game needing a fourth player. I was now an alternate for the Ranch game of bridge.

(2014 update) After a year of filling in I have reached the ranks of 'weekly player'. We now have husbands of some of the women wanting to join in. Two of them have earned the rank, 'Bad Boys of Bridge' and may have t-shirts made to reflect their new status.

The next afternoon found me in the Pavilion getting ready for the weekly Bingo game played by most of the women who participate in the Bunko, San Felipe Rummy and Mexican Dominoes games. Each Ranch game has a small buy-in amount. Bingo costs the most with a fee of $5 going for ten cards each containing six games.

I arrived early at the Pavilion so I could clear my e-mail containing two days worth of advertisements. The political party of my choice constantly asks me to send them $10 or more to stop the other party from taking away my Social Security check and Medicare health plan. A choice needed to be made. The number one plan was to send a check to the party trying to save retirement benefits for everyone in the room. The second plan was to use the money to entertain myself, stay out of the heat and send one of the women home with a few pesos in her pocket. This would make her happy for the next 24 hours. I went with door number two.

Before starting the game, Sandy, the director, asked me if I wanted more than one set of cards to play at the same time. Looking at the sheet of six games needing to be observed with each number called, I let her know the one set would be all I could handle. Maybe the next time I would know if my mind could scan two sheets and mark the numbers before I-22 or whatever number was called next. As the game was played, the one sheet of numbers fulfilled my ability level of number scanning. By the time the last game ended, I knew this was not going to be my regular Friday afternoon pastime. I needed to either save myself for water volleyball or get into a bridge game wanting a fourth. The activity of stamping numbers for two hours did not 'rock my boat'.

The women who do come to play the Bingo games also come to see their friends. Many are not able to participate in other physical activities played at the Ranch. Water aerobics in the pool, walks, a set of tennis or pickle ball are just a few of those activities. I respect their bliss when they can say 'Bingo!' and collect the Ranch bucks for their next meal at the poolside bar or in the Pavilion Restaurant. Bridge would be a better fit for me along with the rummy and domino games.

The weekend arrived and the only games possible would be the pickup events organized by individuals playing either at their homes or in the Pavilion. Water volleyball, played at 12:30 and on certain afternoons at 4:00 P.M. is also an activity played every day and anyone can join. It is now 7:37 A.M. and I am planning on going to the local store, Rancho Market, to try their breakfast special being advertised by the new owner. He is trying a promotion to get the local residents to make his general store a breakfast stop as well.

Sunday has now arrived and many of the residents go to a non-denominational English-speaking church in the town of San Felipe where they can meet others staying for the summer. I have my own beliefs in a higher power, which is inclusive of other life styles and beliefs. I try to live my beliefs by not judging others. I also found out that a Catholic Church offers services in English. I am sure those gringos who make the move to Mexico will find a religious direction that fills their needs. Enough said.

Chapter 28
Everyone Has An Opinion

I attended the opening of the breakfast special at Rancho market. Several Ranch residents attended the event and I shared a table with Nikki and several of her friends. I had played bridge in her condo a few days before. During the breakfast I learned more about her travels and life abroad. She lived in Japan from 1974 to 1979 and practiced nursing part-time at an American school. Her apartment condo contained many of the items from that country, including a wooden Samurai sword used for practice and several wall hangings framed and kept in perfect condition over the years.

Mexican Brick Information: One of the Ranch inhabitants who also worked as a nurse in her career sat next to me. After a few moments of quiet, waiting to see who would start the conversation, we both opened up and found common ground in dialogue about the construction of homes on the Ranch. I told her the home we are renting was painted orange which seemed to take in the heat of the day and radiate it in the night both outward and into the house.

She said the color may have something to do with the night heat but the true culprit lay in the Mexican brick the house was built with. The brick has a lot of air pockets. The air spaces in the material heat up in the day. As the cooler evening arrives, the hot air escapes and goes into the house as well as outside.

I agreed with her and told her how I experienced the brick giving off heat a few nights before when returning from my neighbor's house after sunset. As I approached the house in the cooler air separating the two homes, I was hit with a blast of hot air about five feet from the porch.

The house was probably 15 or 20 degrees warmer than the air only ten feet from its walls and the same heat was pouring into the house.

Now I knew for sure why the area of the house, without the AC on, heated up after nightfall. A home with good insulation would cool as the night temperatures drop and maintain the temperatures within the home through the night. My opinion about Mexican brick, based on what I have seen and experienced is: it makes colorful walkways and porch patios. Because it is one of the cheapest building materials found in Mexico, retaining or patio walls could also be built with the brick. Do not use it for areas needing insulation. This includes garages because all items in this location, including your car, will face the reverse effect of getting hotter at night as the brick releases its hot air.

More Building Information: This is what I have learned about building or buying a house in Mexico. Research the builder and find out what materials they used to construct the home. Windows should be double paned and, if there are any doubts about the home, then see if a neighbor has any information. Most of the time there is someone who was living near the casa as it was being built. They will know what materials were used. If doubt continues to plague your mind, then get permission to drill into the walls and recover a sample of the building material. If it contains foam or a mixture of foam and cement, the chances are the R factor is good. Also, come on a hot day and put your hand on the interior wall and feel the temperature. If the interior walls remain cool when the outside thermometer reaches 102, there is a reasonable chance the house was built with a good insulation material and you will be comfortable in the summer as well as the winter.

Writing a chapter about different people's opinions is something I will leave open and add to as I continue to live down here. Since the book will appear on e-books I can up date the information as it changes, and in Mexico everything changes.

Today is June 26 and I am traveling to Brawley on Thursday for an appointment with a chiropractor at the clinic Suzanne and I discovered soon after we arrived in Baja. There may be a bone adjuster in San Felipe but I have not yet allowed my medical needs to be met in Mexico while I still have Medicare, which pays for this care.

Medical Information: Most of those who are in the age bracket of having Medicare usually travel to California or Arizona to see a physician. If you are located far down in Mexico, Central America or South America, you are now subject to your own research and what you can find. When I visited Lima, Peru in 2006, I found the city to be modern with services suitable to use. I did not need any medical help at the time and I am sure the services lessen as one travels to smaller communities. The cities in Mexico have medical practitioners, and I would feel comfortable if I needed to visit a doctor in Mexicali or even San Felipe. Where I live now, a medical doctor is located in a small clinic on the Ranch. Residents are allowed two medical check-ups a year paid through their HOA dues. If something more serious happens, a helicopter medical insurance can be purchased. Instead of a two-hour drive to California a half-hour flight can make all the difference if a serious condition flares up or an accident happens to a resident.

A few residents who have not yet reached the Medicare age have purchased Mexican health insurance and are under the protection of the medical doctors either in San Felipe or Mexicali. The ones I have talked to seem fine with the medical coverage costing around $240 a month. My wife, Suzanne, is still using her medical coverage from the Flagstaff Unified School

District, but she has to travel to Arizona or California to use it. She purchases her medications and sees a doctor north of the border, and pays around $350 a month in monthly premiums. She has a little more than a year before she is eligible for Medicare and the benefit package it allows her.

I know the medical issues are different for everyone and a high priority for many people thinking of moving to Mexico either as a Snowbird or a full-time resident. My observation and comment is this: Research the area where you are moving. Many medical doctors in larger communities have received training in the States. Find out from the Canadians or Americans where you are planning on living how they handle their medical needs. Because we live so close to the border, the drive to California or Arizona is not stressful for us at the moment. For those Yankees moving further into Mexico the medical issues need more attention and more answers.

More Documents

Because I have let many people know I am writing a book about making the move to Mexico and the different hurdles one faces after moving here, I have received many requests as to what I need to inform the reader about. I will list them here and discuss them to the best of my ability.

1. Land ownership and the Fideicomiso.
2. Getting a Sentri pass across the border.
3. Passport card

Fideicomiso

I have copied a description of what a Fideicomiso is and how it works. The information is from the Playa de Oro web page and I feel their description is the easiest to understand. There were several other web pages but they were written in terms meant for a lawyer and we all know how those read.

WHAT IT IS AND HOW IT WORKS
Foreigners acquire irrevocable and absolute ownership rights to property in Mexico through a 50-year perpetually renewable and transferable Bank Trust called a Fideicomiso. This Trust is a legal substitute for deeded (commonly referred to in the U.S. as fee simple) ownership and is provided *specifically* for non-nationals to own property in the formerly restricted zones (border and beach areas.) The Trust system of ownership is sanctioned by the Mexican government,

provided for under the Mexican Constitution, and secured by the Central Bank of Mexico; thereby offering powerful protection.

THE MECHANICS Title is delivered to a Mexican Bank, authorized to act as the Trustee, designating the foreign buyer as the Beneficiary of the Trust (you). The Bank acts like an "employee" of the Beneficiary (you) in transactions involving the property. The Beneficiary (you) retains the use and control of the property and makes all the investment decisions. The rights of use and enjoyment, leasing, improving, mortgaging, selling, inheriting and willing the property is the same as when owned in fee simple title. It is your Trust and not the property of the government or the Bank.

A sale becomes registered when it is witnessed and recorded through a Notorio Publico in Mexicali. From there, title passes to the designated Bank to be held in the Fideicomiso (Trust). There are specific Banks authorized by the Mexican government to hold the Real Estate Fideicomiso. Authorized Banks must pass extreme scrutiny. (Playa de Oro uses BITAL Bank. You, however, have the right to transfer the Fideicomiso to any authorized Bank of your choice.)

The Bank reviews all paperwork of the current owner/developer to ensure that the documents are complete and legal. The Bank will not issue a developer the right to apply for and form the Fideicomiso on their lots until they are satisfied with all documents and that the subdivision process has been completed. A question that often arises - in the event the holding Bank should ever fail, be bought by an unauthorized Bank, etc., what happens to the Fideicomiso? Answer - the Fideicomiso will be transferred to another authorized Bank. The Bank does not own the Fideicomiso, you do!

Unless a problem occurs because of fraud or misrepresentation, the Fideicomiso cannot be compromised (this is where title insurance provides the additional protection necessary for 100% peace of mind - Playa de Oro provides it!)

Foreigners often worry about their land being appropriated by the Mexican government. Under the North American Free Trade Agreement, NAFTA, Mexico may not directly, or indirectly, appropriate property except for a public purpose. This is the same as "Eminent Domain" in the U.S. Where it is necessary to appropriate land, swift and fair market value compensation must be paid, together with accrued interest.

SOME FACTS YOU SHOULD KNOW In 1997, Mexico changed its' Banking system and subscribed to the International Banking Standards. Currently, there is only one Mexican owned Bank left. The rest are owned by different international Banks including Citi Bank and Chase Manhattan.

In the U.S. there are many types of Bank Trusts; living, education, family etc., so are there several types of Fideicomiso for education, for the protection of minors, and for land usage called a Land Usage Trust that allows for the use of the land only. This is commonly set up for Ejido leases between an Ejido and a developer who will in turn, lease portions of the land through a membership program to others. (Membership selling is common practice in Mexico. Be sure to check your documents thoroughly.) There is only ONE Fideicomiso to purchase property called a Real Estate Fideicomiso.

The Real Estate Fideicomiso has been offered either through a Master Trust or Individual Trust. The Fideicomiso offered through Playa de Oro is an individual Fideicomiso, the most secure form of Real Estate Fideicomiso available.

Why is an individual Fideicomiso considered the best? The Beneficiary (you) maintains complete control over the trust (to buy, sell or mortgage, encumber, will or inherit) and is not tied to a Master Trust, which could be compromised with a lien or default by the developer i.e. as in non-payment of taxes. In a Master Trust the developer is responsible for payment of taxes then appropriating them for reimbursement proportionately to each Fideicomiso held under the Master Trust. In an Individual Fideicomiso, every Beneficiary (you) is responsible for payment of their own taxes. A non-payment by one property owner would not affect another property holder in the development. For this reason, most, if not all, Banks are now only issuing Individual Fideicomisos and will no longer approve Master Trusts.

DO MEXICAN BUYERS/SELLERS HAVE SPECIAL DISPENSATION UNDER THE LAW? Whether Mexican or American owned, each development must complete the subdivision process and the only way to sell property to non-nationals is through a Fideicomiso. Mexican developers DO NOT have any special dispensation under the law. If you do not have a Fideicomiso through an authorized Bank then you have, at best, a lease. Any other form of "ownership" such as share of a corporation, squatters (yes, you can even get hit up for this!), owning with a Mexican national partner, or any other gimmick is not legal and is trying to circumvent the law! Mexican nationals own property Deeded but even they cannot own in a subdivision unless the development is properly documented and subdivided. Whether one lot or a thousand lots, in the eyes of the government whenever a parcel is "sub-divided" it must go through the subdivision process.

REMEMBER: The law is very specific about the Real Estate Fideicomiso. This Fideicomiso is designed specifically for non-nationals to own land in the formerly restricted areas (beach, border region) and is the ONLY legal way to own this land. It provides the same legal rights and protection of ownership as a Mexican has under the law. It bestows upon the Beneficiary of the Trust (you) absolute and irrevocable control over the property. The Fideicomiso is set in 50-year increments *guaranteed* renewable for perpetuity. It can be improved, mortgaged, bought, sold, inherited & willed. Playa De Oro offers irrevocable land ownership through an INDIVIDUAL Fideicomiso and absolute

guaranteed protection through **First American Title Insurance Company.**
(Fideicomiso)

SENTRI PASS

A SENTRI pass is a document allowing the driver of a car to cross the border in minutes using a special car lane instead of waiting for 30 to 90 minutes in the mass crossing section of the border. Again, I have gone to the Internet to get a good definition of what it is and how it works. We are presently applying for such a pass to speed up our trip into California from Mexico.

What is the SENTRI program?
The SENTRI (Secure Electronic Network for Travelers Rapid Inspection) program, launched by US Customs and Border Protection, are dedicated commuter lanes where prescreened applicants and vehicles are allowed to cross the border Northbound into the US usually more quickly and efficiently. The enrollees have been rigorously background checked and have been determined to be a low risk to the security of the US border. As one approaches the inspection area, photos and information are given to the inspector about the driver, passengers and vehicle from the SENTRI decal on the vehicle and the information on the SENTRI Portpass or

Passport card. A secondary inspection is randomly determined by computer or if the inspector senses something suspicious.

How do the SENTRI lanes work?
As you approach the inspection station, your SENTRI Portpass card or cards will need to be read by the electronic equipment. You will see a sign showing you where to point the cards. Hold the cards out the window toward the equipment. Since your vehicle decal is permanently applied to your windshield, the equipment will also read it and send the information to the officer. Once you approach the officer, hold out your SENTRI Portpass card or cards to him or her. (Sentri Pass)

Passport Card

I have copied the web page information regarding Passport cards for the reader.

The U.S. Passport Card can be used to enter the United States from Canada, Mexico, the Caribbean, and Bermuda at land border crossings or sea ports-of-entry and is more convenient and less expensive than a passport book. **The passport card cannot be used for international travel by air.**

Validity and Cost

Adults (Age 16 and Older) Validity: 10 years
Minors (Under Age 16) Validity: 5 years

First-Time Application Cost: $55
Cost for All Minors: $40

How To Apply
All U.S. citizens may apply for a passport card. If you have a U.S. passport book and are eligible to use Form DS-82, you may apply for the card by mail. You can use Form DS-82 to renew your passport book at the same time that you apply for your passport card.

If you have never had a U.S. passport book or are not eligible to use Form DS-82, you must apply in person for DS-11.

All passport cards will be returned using First Class Mail. Passport cards cannot be shipped to you using overnight delivery.

Security
To increase speed, efficiency, and security at U.S. land and sea border crossings, the passport card contains a vicinity-read radio frequency identification (RFID) chip. **There is no**

personal information written to the RFID chip. This chip points to a stored record in secure government databases.

With RFID technology, Customs and Border Protection inspectors will be able to access photographs and other biographical information stored in secure government databases as the traveler approaches an inspection station.
The passport card uses **state-of-the-art security features** to prevent the possibility of counterfeiting and forgery. A protective RFID-blocking sleeve is provided with each passport card to protect against unauthorized reading or tracking of the card when it is not in use.

The only drawback for those wanting a passport card is this, if you are already living in Mexico: The card takes a minimum of three weeks to obtain and you have to send off your passport with the application. In other words if you send in the application while in Mexico you have no passport to travel back to the States. It might be a better idea to send for the card when you have a longer period of time in the States. I would rather have the card and my passport sent to me at an address in the States instead of in Mexico. That is my feeling, and maybe others who have lived in Mexico for a longer period of time may have a different attitude regarding the mail service to Mexico. The best solution is to get the card before you move to Mexico. There is now a faster lane for the card at the new crossing in Mexicali. (Passport Card)

Chapter 29
What To Do in July and August

Suzanne and I have now been gone from the Ranch for several weeks visiting relatives in Ramona, CA and a college friend in Laguna Beach, CA. Because we are renting a house with such poor insulation, trips to the Pacific Coast and cooler weather are necessary. If we buy a house next year, we will make sure the R factor in the house is sufficient and the windows are double-paned to help keep out the heat. The prices in our development for many houses up for sale are low and some great deals are available. With a good insulated house the summers are much more comfortable.

Many residents with well-insulated homes do stay all summer and focus on indoor projects during the day. They may visit others and socialize within the walls of a friend's insulated home or participate in the games set up for the summer, either at the pool or the tables within the different buildings on the Ranch.

Developments along the Pacific side of Baja do not have the heat to contend with in the summer. The Pacific Ocean with the morning fog conditions keeps the coastal temperatures at a manageable level. The trade-off is the cost of living may be higher on the west coast of Baja and the weather is much cooler in the winter months. The Sea of Cortez side of Baja is usually in the mid 60's to 70's in the day, while other locations drop to lower temperatures in December and January.

What we plan to do next summer is travel. If we have a home, we will shut it down and head to our families in California and Oregon. We may even explore areas of the northern states we have never visited. These include Idaho, Canada, North Dakota and the New England areas. We also have close friends in Flagstaff, and at 7000 feet in elevation, the town is a perfect place to visit in the warm summer months.

From the description I have given, it appears we are becoming Snowbirds. We are no longer living in a cold climate in the winter and we will be leaving the extreme conditions of heat in the summer and flying north to enjoy the cooler weather. It makes sense to us, and I do see why a large population in the States makes such a move twice a year.

I have mentioned before that not everyone in Baja leaves for the summer. I was told that around 15% of the total Ranch population stays for the hot months. Some may not have relatives to visit during the summer. Others may love the heat and playing water volleyball, while some may not have a choice but to stick it out during the two or three months of heat and humidity. There are a few people who stay and earn a little income watering the plants of those who are gone for the summer. A few residents house-sit for others, staying in beautiful homes, watering plants, and caring for any animals left in Mexico while the owners are away.

There are people who live in solar areas of the Ranch and may not have enough energy to run an AC unit in July and August. A fan is usually not enough to stay cool, so these are the residents available to housesit and care for other homes. Many residents seem to have made close connections with each other either through the social gatherings or various events held during the year. They watch out for each other on the Ranch. Other communities are probably similar throughout Mexico.

Travel in Mexico: The description of Baja sums up the possibilities of July and August if you decide to live in the warm climates of Mexico. I have read that other towns and cities in Mexico are located at higher elevations and have milder climates in the summer. Mexico City is at an elevation of 7350 ft., even higher than Flagstaff, Arizona but situated closer to the equator. After viewing the weather in Mexico City online, it seems the best time to travel to the capital is in April and May. The temperatures are in the upper 70s and the rainfall is one inch or less. During June, July and August, the temperatures drop due to the rainy season and most of the days are wet. If one wants to visit a town on the mainland of Mexico, Google or Bing the weather and see if the rainy season is in the summer. April and May could turn out to be the better time to travel throughout our southern neighbor.

Chapter 30
Alternative Medicine

As I am writing this part of the book, we are preparing to return to El Centro and Brawley for a last bit of food shopping, another doctor visit to see results of blood work for Suzanne, and receive an acupuncture treatment for me. The doctor doing the acupuncture in Brawley charges half of what the doctor charged in Phoenix. I have seen signs for acupuncture doctors in Mexicali but I have not checked into them and to discovered what they charge. The treatment for sticking needles into my body is not covered by Medicare. The insurance would cover the medication treatment for numbness in the legs but not the natural way of helping blood and energy flow to the lower limbs through this ancient Chinese method. What could the Chinese possibly know? They have been treating people with this system for thousands of years versus a drug company that has been around for only 20 years with their pill-form of a cure. I sure wish the medical field in America would catch up to non-medical treatments that have worked for centuries instead of the 'Drugs R Us' approach.

My visit to Dr. Almaden, the acupuncture specialist, turned out to be a good connection with an alternative practitioner. After dropping Suzanne off at her appointment at the Clinical de Saluda del Pueblo, I went to the small office complex for alternative healing about two blocks away. Paper work had to be filled out, and the information contained a series of questions regarding mental, physical and emotional health. Each question had to be given a value of 1 to 3 depending upon how one judged their own make-up in those areas. I answered as honestly as I could, knowing if Suzanne had the honor of grading me the scores might be different. Wives and husbands see their significant other differently in many areas. I felt my responses filled the bill and gave the doctor what he needed.

After the weigh-in and height stats were taken and blood pressure measured, I was taken to a room and waited for Dr. Almaden to arrive. In a few minutes, a man with Chinese features, short graying hair and the physical stature of a small linebacker at the college level of football, entered the room wearing a black shirt with Hawaiian designs. Without an introduction he simply started to go through the questionnaire I had filled out and asked more in-depth questions regarding physical concerns.

"Do you have urination problems?" he asked.

"Yes, I have to stop and go a lot," was my reply.

"Why do you think that is happening?" was his next question.

"Old age?" was my question and answer.

The questioning continued with a few of the words needing more translation because English was not Dr. Almaden's first language. I knew he was not of Mexican descent because his accent had given me the needed clues and by now I could tell an English-speaking Mexican accent from a mile away.

"Please sit here on the patient's table and give me your arm," was the next direction.

I sat and held out my arm as he started to take my pulse. By the way he held my arm and used all his fingers to feel the different pulse areas, I knew he was using the ancient eastern method of deep pulse reading. This method is used by Chinese and Indian practitioners and taught today to those who want to learn it through a healing method called Ayurvedic medicine. Suzanne studied the method from her chiropractor, Dr. Helen, in Santa Rosa, California. Dr. Helen learned the practice through a study group started by Deepak Chopra. He is the famed Indian doctor who has written many books including ones about the ancient art of healing.

As he took my pulse he asked me, "Do your kidneys bother you?"

I answered "no" and he continued on to other areas of my body while holding my arm and reading the information my pulse was giving him. I asked him if he was practicing the Chinese method of pulse reading and he confirmed my observation. From then on he seemed to become more open to me. I believe it had to do with the fact that I knew something about alternative medicine. I even mentioned the name of the Dalai Lama because I knew his medical practitioners used this same method of diagnosis when treating him.

Kundun is a great movie about the early life of the spiritual leader of Tibet. One can see the health practitioners using the same pulse reading technique in the movie. Any treatment good enough for the Noble Peace Prize winner and exiled leader of the Tibetan nation is good enough for me.

My previous treatment with a "pin" doctor was in Phoenix. After three sessions the numbness in my lower legs lessened tremendously. I knew the same such treatment would again allow the energy and circulation flow to return to its normal rate without the western medicine in pill form. Libby and many other drug companies claim an instant fix to all human ailments. If the reader senses I am not convinced that western medicine is the answer to human health conditions, you would be right.

The treatment consisted of needles placed in areas of energy centers throughout my legs, and electric impulse wires were attached. I could feel the vibrations of the shocks throughout my lower legs and even through my upper body. I was told to relax and Dr. Almaden said he would be checking in on me in 20 minutes to make sure I was all right. The light went off and I took a short nap, much needed after being zapped by the 98-degree heat of Brawley.

The two weeks on the Pacific Ocean in temperatures only reaching 80 degrees refreshed us. At the same time, the cool weather weakened our resistance to the extreme heat of the Imperial Valley and what we would soon be facing in San Felipe when we returned in the morning.

After the treatment was completed I asked the doctor if I could ask him a personal question. He agreed. I asked him where he came from. The Philippines was his answer. Even though he came from that island nation, I was sure Chinese was his biological origin. I thanked him for his treatment and met his wife as I was leaving. She also looked Chinese but spoke English without an accent. She was gracious and friendly and I knew I had found a good alternative medical practitioner for half the price of the Phoenix "pin" doctor. Brawley was working out rather well for me in the field of alternative health practices.

The short walk to the clinic where Suzanne was staying was uneventful but warm. By now the large meal we had for breakfast was digested and no longer filled our stomachs. We had not eaten since 9 a.m. in Julian, a small hillside community 22 miles east of Ramona. This is a place both Suzanne and I went to with our parents when we were growing up in the San Diego area. The old stores and hotels were kept in pristine condition and ready to serve the many tourists with food and collectibles for the home, reminding them of their visit to this small frontier town of the 1800's. The huge homemade pancake with nuts and apples along with a couple of eggs no longer kept the pangs of hunger away.

We both decided to eat first before seeing the movie called *The Help*. We love movies and try to catch the one with the biggest buzz when we head up to California on a doctor visit or a food run. The theater, located between Brawley and El Cento, listed our movie start time as 4 p.m.

and 7 p.m. We just missed the first showing and had three hours until the later performance.

Questions regarding our AT&T phones and a recommended Italian restaurant in the new mall across the highway from El Centro guided us towards nourishment and communication answers. After our meal we gave Carino's two thumbs up, and we will be returning again with friends when we show off our hunting and gathering skills regarding good places to eat. A quick visit to AT&T still left us with one and a half hours before show time. We decided *The Help* could wait and headed back to the AC-cooled hotel room to unwind and prepare for the errands of the next day.

Suzanne had received a small computer from her brother, Michael, while we were in Ramona. He usually owns the latest in computer technology and the small HP no longer fit his needs. We now each have our own computers and we spent the next hour answering e-mails and keeping up with the latest news provided by Google. An evening movie on the tube rounded out our entertainment and by 9 p.m. we were asleep.

The drug store, Chase Bank and Vons shopping filled the morning schedule while the temperature remained in the high 80's. By noon we were crossing the border on our way back to El Dorado Ranch and the heat of August. The road was still being worked on. From what I could tell a whole new section was being prepared for the job of putting drainage pipes under and bridges over highway 5. Side roads were being constructed to divert the traffic and allow the work to be done. Either the Mexican government knows something about the weather the rest of the world does not know and is preparing for the great flood of the century, or it has extra cash for infrastructure building and it is putting a large number of people to work. I hoped that eventually the sidewalks, streets and curbs in many of the towns and cities in Baja would also be on the list of things to fix.

It was Thursday and the 4 p.m. social was being held at the house of another one of the single women living on the Ranch. Sandy's home was located just off the golf course and across from one of the pools on the Ranch, used to provide water for irrigation on the eighteen holes of grass. We arrived home with just enough time to fill up with gas, unload the car and proceed to the gathering. Retirement does not mean you have nothing to do. We wanted to visit Sandy's house and were not disappointed. The cooler weather San Felipe was having at the moment allowed us to sit on the porch overlooking the golf course and enjoy a cool drink. We snacked on the finger foods provided by each person coming to the event.

Suzanne and I were still the newbie couple and at this stage of our existence on the Ranch we spent a lot of time listening to the newest developments and what each occupant thought about how things were getting done. The new swimming pool was under construction at the time and already petitions were being signed as to how each group wanted the lap pool to look. The contractor was doing it his way and not the way it was planned. Different views also were discussed as to how the pool on the ocean side of the Ranch was being shared with the families of the employees. The heat of summer made the swimming areas a top priority in discussions. Probably the subject would not end until winter when the pool population dwindled and most people spent their time in other outdoor activities involving travel and exploring the area.

An early evening at home followed the social event, and again we found the bed by 9 p.m. The following morning Oscar from Fix It Express arrived to again look at the refrigerator. The box was not in the same cooling mode it had been when I left 2 weeks before. An hour later a new thermostat replaced the old one and faith was again restored in the keeper of our food items. A quick trip into town to exchange dollars for pesos at our bank and a stop at the Telcel store to recharge the telephone minutes completed our business for the day. We had enough time to use our computers at the pool, swim for an hour and head to Pete's Camp for the weekly celebration honoring whom ever had had a birthday during the previous week.

Pete's Camp is a development located right next to the Ranch. It has a bar and restaurant so close to the water one could get enough salt for their meal by simply holding their plate above their head, allowing the ocean breeze blowing in from the Sea of Cortez to douse the meal with the needed spice. The Mexican-American eatery provided the perfect place for such a gathering. The cooler weather continued and the almost full- moon rising out of the Gulf of California rounded out the evening for those attending the event.

Home again and in bed by 9:30. Our next event was the monthly full moon barbeque and bocce ball tournament held on the beach of El Dorado. I believe the tournament was started to satisfy the Italian residents and enable them to show their bowling skills. I decided to wear my NY baseball hat I had bought on the streets of the

Big Apple several years before to honor the large Italian population present in all areas of New York. We were told to be at the event by 5:00 and to bring a dish to share. The hot dogs would not be ready until 7:00, so anytime between those hours would be fine.

The busy schedule of going to the pool to read our e-mail, swimming and doing a little shopping at the local grocery store tired us out a bit so we decided to be an observer of the bocce ball tournament and arrive at a later time. At 6:30 we drove up to the crowded parking lot and discovered the information we had received was not all true. At 5:00 the potluck meal was eaten. After the meal the tournament begins. The balls had just begun to roll on the hard-surfaced sand with a rope used to outline the course. No requirements of having ever played the game were needed. We decided to get some food first and then watch the game as it unfolded in the waning light of the day. With the Sea of Cortez as a backdrop and the expected full-moon scheduled to appear within the hour, the stage was set for continued fun in our new home in Mexico. The cooler weather still held and the ocean breezes allowed the event to be played out in the low 80's.

Gary and his wife Jean turned out to be the winners for the Italian ball game, and I suspect the two were not new to this sport. Gary seemed to know how to put the needed backspin on the ball allowing it to end up near the marker and win the needed points. Anyone rolling the ball played at the mercy of the hard packed ground and rocks guiding the sphere to a completely different location than the one intended. Techniques employed included the Gary Italian back spin, power rolls to knock out the opponents' position near the marker ball and the old "bounce off the rope used to mark the course" trick, hoping a lucky rock would guide the ball to the point-winning position near the marker. Everyone seemed to be having fun, so next month the Jeff and Suzanne team will be taking up the great Italian sport second only to soccer and maybe eating. Food is almost a sport in Italy, and if you ever ate a full coarse meal in that country you would know what I mean.

Full moon rising over Sea of Cortez during bocce ball tournament

A comment needs to be made to honor the activities team, David, Tako, Mario and Jorge, who co-ordinate all the top events held at different times of the day. The water volleyball is the 12:30 ritual held at the pool. Different card and dominoes events are also managed by some of the team members. The young men are always in attendance and work many hours to keep the summer crowd happy with fun and games.

I can only imagine what the crowd numbers will increase to when cooler weather prevails and the Snowbirds return. I have heard the Mexican Train Dominoes tables can be as many as 12 with six people at a table. Bingo must also be huge. The last Bingo game is a winner-take-all and it cost a dollar to play. If 150 people play, the lucky blackout cardholder may walk away with enough cash to fill their propane tank for three months.

Today is Sunday the 14th of August, and we have decided to do some relaxing at the pool after we caught up with the laundry piled up from our trip and stay in San Diego. We are going to our neighbor's house tonight for another dinner gathering. Ed, my neighbor, has been a bachelor for several weeks while his wife, Suzanne, cools off in Ensenada. Ed is the gardener of the house, and water is needed for the many plants and trees in their yard, which make it an oasis. He is a good source of information as well as a good neighbor and always guides me to the many different providers in San Felipe with whom he has had good results. Things like a mechanic, good restaurants and what days to shop for fruits and vegetables are always good things to know when living in a country lacking the conveniences of a Jiffy Lube, Olive Garden or the produce section of Vons.

We plan to be in San Felipe until the 24th of August, when we again return to Brawley for follow up medical appointments and a quick return to Ramona. From there we will plan a return route to San Felipe by going to San Diego and cross the border at Tijuana. Neither

Suzanne nor I have been to this border town for many years and we do not plan on staying. Tijuana has been in the news several times for people getting caught trafficking drugs. The reputation of the community puts it into a category of a city not desirable for a long visit. Ensenada is our destination and we expect to find weather conditions similar Laguna Beach. We stayed four nights visiting our friends George and Kathy in a beautiful timeshare development overlooking the Pacific Ocean.

Chapter 31
Water Volleyball, The Summer Religion

Yesterday the date was August 18, 2011 and I played water volleyball for the first time in four years. I have been putting it off due to the fact I did not know how my right knee or back would hold up. We arrived at the pool early to check our e-mail and get in a swim, because the temperature was going to reach 102 degrees and already the humidity was causing me to sweat. My tee shirt turned into a wet rag just from the act of breathing. If a person is at the pool before 12:00 and they look like they can stand in water and hit volleyball, then they are asked if they want to be on one of the teams playing a round-robin style tournament held each and every day at 12:30 sharp. On this hot and humid day I finally gave in and agreed to be on one of the teams.

Water Volleyball played daily, rain or shine

At this date in August, most of those who are going to leave due to the high humidity and heat have already done so. Even with the large numbers of Ranch residents gone, enough locals and visitors showed up to create four teams with six players on each team. The net and rope markers were put into place around 12:29 and the first two teams entered the water. One team on a shallow side and the other team in deeper water with the back line around 4.5 feet in depth. Smaller women and men, some barely over five feet in height, have to move towards the net when their team is in the deep end. If they served the ball in the deepest part of the court, only their head would appear above the water and their arms would remain submerged, stopping them from completing a serve to the other court. The team in the shallow end of the pool usually has the advantage depending upon which players are playing at the time.

The team in the deep end always gets to serve first due to the water depth disadvantage. Easy points can be made when a short player has to come close to the net thus leaving an open area between them and the back rope. On the shallow side of the court tall players take advantage of their height and direct smashes blast into the opposite court after a perfect set is made. During the afternoon games, beer and other poolside drinks are downed, thus taking the edge off the high humidity and warmer weather of August.

Humor increases in the later games because of the drinking during the waiting period between games. After one woman made a good hit to one of her net players he was able to smash the ball and win a point. Another player on her team complimented her by saying, "Good set."

In volleyball this term means the player returned the ball to one of their teammates just in front of the net thus enabling the teammate to hit a hard spike and win a point. The woman instantly placed her hands under her boobs, lifted them up and said, "Thank you for noticing."

After a minute of uncontrollable laughter, the players, who heard the comment, were again ready to play. Many of the women at the Ranch who play this water sport are fifty or older and have either lost most of their inhibitions at that age or by the third game are too drunk to care. With this player, whose name I shall never repeat due to the fact she may kick my ass if I did, both factors may have come into play.

I survived six games with my shoulders and face covered in #30 sunscreen accompanied by dark glasses and a hat. I felt good being on a team with four wins and two losses, and I knew I could do this again after a few days. Suzanne and I returned home. I took a painkiller and a nap and relaxed the rest of the day. Recovery was now in progress.

The next morning I awoke and felt no pain in my back or neck areas. These are parts of my body, which show the first signs that I may have over done it in the area of exercise. Most of the regular players of this water sport go to the pool every day. I was not ready to make such a commitment and knew I needed a day or two in between playing to make sure nothing was stretched too far.

I enjoyed the exercise and knew this pool activity could replace walking. Suzanne was not able to do her morning ritual at sunrise due to a damaged right knee. She believes she may have torn a ligament in the kneecap area and continued to do more damage to it by stepping in a hole while on a walk. She again hurt it while attempting an hour of water aerobics.

(2014 update) The new pool is finished. The ribbon cutting ceremony was held in May of 2013, and the first game of water volleyball was played. There is now a pool made for this water sport as well as water aerobics, which is done in the early morning. The big new pool has lap lanes and easy to access at any time. The hot-tub pool is also quite nice. The new pool is a big bonus for the Ranch and was built by the HOA dues collected over the years.

Ask Questions: Many retired folk on the Ranch or in other communities in Mexico may not participate in such a physical activity as water volleyball, but those who can, generally do. Along with the residents are the vacationers who own land or a house in the development and are at the pool enjoying the lifestyle of swimming and having lunch or drinks. I drink very little in Mexico and there are many like me, so do not think everyone down here indulges. For those who do like to have beer and other drinks either by the pool or on their porch in the evenings, there are many in Mexico who will join you. We are all adults and we all make our own choices.

Being at the pool is a good time to seek out and meet some of those who have made this area their home. Try to engage them in between games and maybe talk to someone on your team if you decide to play. Try to find out more about the area you are in before the third and fourth games because many of the players enjoy drinking a beer or two while playing, and the more intelligent and in-depth answers will come to you during the first few rounds of water volleyball.

Chapter 32
Continued Daily Life in Mexico

A few days ago Suzanne commented that one of my teeth appeared to be getting darker. I had been putting off returning to the first dentist I visited when I came down to San Felipe last March. I had my teeth cleaned at that time and a routine checkup cost me $30. The checkup reported two fillings needing replacement and a possible cavity. The tooth turning dark could mean it was dying and visions of having to get it pulled filled my head and increased my fear factor. I called and made an appointment with another dentist, recommended to me by a resident in the area who worked at the Roadrunner Café. She spoke highly of this woman dentist, so I decided to give her a try.

The day I called was one of the hottest days of summer, with high humidity. I made an appointment for 10 a.m. the next morning so the heat factor would not wipe me out. Going into town in the afternoon was out of the question. Now that I have been living here for several months, buildings and other landmarks are familiar to me when I am given directions to a location in town.

"Turn right at the road that takes you to the airport and go to the first stop sign. There is a nursery on the corner. Turn left and she is in the strip mall on your right."

I arrived at 10 and sat across from another American waiting to have her teeth checked. I asked her if she had been to Dr. Lexa before. She confirmed she and her whole family see Dr.

Lexa and her husband, Dr. Jason who is also a dentist in the same office. Not only are they both dentists, Jason also does orthodontia and straightens teeth. While filling out the new patient form, I asked the woman in the waiting room if the date was the 19th. She looked at me with a blank stare and answered,

"I don't know. If I do not turn on my computer in the morning I usually do not have any idea of the date or what day of the week it is."

We both started to laugh and acknowledged we were both victims of being retired. While living in Mexico, we do not need to know the day of the week or date unless an appointment was in the near future.

The woman was soon escorted into the office. She had her appointment with Dr. Jason. Within a few minutes I was directed to the other dental chair in the same room. The dental office was modern looking and all the equipment appeared new and in excellent working condition.

Dr. Lexa spoke fairly good English. Within minutes of her asking me what I did when I worked, she found out I was a teacher. She started asking my advice about education and topics including home school and whether or not it was a good idea. I told her about my wife's daughter who home-schooled her four children but she did not work at an outside job. Teaching children, to learn about the world is a full-time job, and if the parent has the time and the skill, the results can be positive. Since Dr. Lexa works each day, going home and teaching her children may be a lot on her plate, and the results may not be as good as if she did not work. She agreed she needed downtime after looking into mouths of patients all day. The teachers at school would have to do the education job for now.

I let Dr. Lexa know my father was a dentist. I seem to pass on this bit of information to the dentists I use. It is probably done as an act of self-defense, so they will be extra careful while poking around my mouth with sharp instruments. I also explain to the dentists I meet why I decided not to join the profession like my father. As a young boy I used to look through the dental books my dad used when he was a student and see the pictures of different mouths with the accompanying diseases a set of teeth, might incur if not properly managed. It was enough to steer me away from dentistry and all other medical professions involving bodily fluids and blood.

After checking my teeth Dr. Lexa explained to me what was happening to the tooth, which appeared to be getting darker. The older filling beneath the newer clear filling was starting to send the color of silver under the clear filling. Nothing needed to be done and there were no new cavities. She asked me if I wanted to have my teeth cleaned now and I said "yes." I felt relief. My mind had started to play out scenarios the day before when I made the appointment. Having the tooth, which appeared to be dead pulled, and having to get several cavities filled was not something I looked forward to. I decided at that moment Dr. Lexa would be my dentist during the duration of my stay in San Felipe.

Dental and Medical Information: Finding the best doctor or dentist in Mexico and in the States is crucial. You may have to try out several to get one that fits you as an individual. Do not be misdirected by those in the States who say the dentists and doctors in Mexico are no good. This is more of the misinformation campaign waged by those who think they know everything about Mexico because they once heard a horror story from a friend of a friend ten years ago. I have found both medical and dental services to be up to the standard of those found in the States.

By the time the cleaning was finished and Dr. Lexa had sung several songs during the process, I felt relaxed and at ease. Singing seems to be something common with the Mexican population while they are working. The guy who fixed our refrigerator sang several songs during the time spent getting cool air to circulate around our perishables. Now I have a singing dentist who actually has a good voice. I thanked her and mentioned I was writing a book about my move to San Felipe and my experiences while adjusting to the lifestyle in El Dorado. She laughed and said I should also include my trip to the dentist. I told her I would be including her and the experience while at the office.

"If I include you in the book, then I can get you to buy it," I told her.

I left the office after paying 350 pesos or $29 dollars for the cleaning and checkup and headed to a restaurant called Georges Café where an American breakfast was served. Pancakes and a couple of eggs over easy became my mini-celebration for having no major dental work needed. The breakfast stop also gave me time to call Suzanne and write down a few items I could get from the food market, DJ's. I mentioned before that the store caters to American food needs with things like Rice Dream, a non-dairy milk product, and many different kinds of breakfast cereals. Some long time residents who have shopped there said they found his prices a little high. If DJ's is the only store supplying some of the things we like and the only other place to purchase these items is in El Centro, the little extra cost is well worth it.

I returned home with the temperatures starting to rise again. We were in another hot spell, and a trip to the pool was necessary on such days. We still use Wi-FI at the Ranch, and now we both have our own computers. The process of answering our individual e-mails is quicker and getting into the water comes sooner.

On Friday night we again went to the social gathering held in at Pete's Camp. We went last week to celebrate a birthday and this week Suzanne just wanted to get out and talk to those locals who make the Ranch their home. Several new people, whom I had only seen at the pool, attended the gathering. I met Tom, who also went to the same college, Univ. of California at Santa Barbara, several years before me. He worked in the field of special needs with boys and girls in a group home near the UCSB campus. I taught the same population in group homes in the Santa Rosa area of California, so we had several stories to swap.

Another gentleman, Bob, seemed to be a person with great depth and knowledge about the workings of the Ranch. He serves on various committees working to move things along on the Ranch. The more I talked to him, the more I knew he would be another 'go to' guy if I needed more information about a subject or where to go in order to get something I wanted. When I asked him if I could use his name in the book, he said he was living here under the 'Witness Protection Program' and Bob was not his real name. Like I have said throughout the book, there are some real funny people living down here.

Chapter 33
Certain People Should Not Move to Mexico

Yesterday was August 24, 2011, and both Suzanne and I saw the movie, "The Help," while in El Centro for a doctor's visit. This movie was so moving. I felt I needed to pass on information to the readers who are thinking of Mexico as a place to relocate. The setting for the film was in Jackson, Mississippi and the time period was in the early '60s. A book was put together by the maids telling the stories and experiences of being hired help in this southern town, describing the attitudes and racial prejudices held by the white women for whom they worked.

The time period took place during my high-school years, and even in California such attitudes existed to a lesser degree. The movie described the fear-based ideas being passed around by the women of this southern society while playing their weekly bridge game. Building separate bathrooms for the help came about due to the unfounded fears regarding diseases only the black population carried. These diseases could be passed on to the white population through shared toilet use.

Third-World Attitudes: These attitudes of looking down on other cultures and races still exist in the world. A person who holds such feelings need not apply to the "Move to Mexico Club" or other third-world countries. I can save you a lot of pain. The experience of living here will not be an enjoyable one. There are a few individuals who have moved to San Felipe who think the Mexicans are inferior, make jokes about them and have little to do with the culture other than drinking Mexican beer and using the local population to clean their houses and fix appliances. No attempt is made by them to learn the language, engage in the culture or even travel throughout the country. This causes me to question, "Why are they here?"

This is a wake-up call for the reader who may be thinking of such a move. Visit and stay in the community where you may relocate. Give yourself a gut check.

'Do you despise or look down upon the population of the country surrounding you?'

If you do and you see no possibility of changing your attitudes towards the locals and their lifestyle then maybe another country would be a better fit. Outer Mongolia might be just the place. The Mexican population or any Latin American country does not need anymore "Ugly Americans" coming to their communities. Some Americans come to these countries to help the population become just like them. **The truth is most Mexicans do not want to become just like us. The Mexican population may be poor in material goods but they are not poor in spirit. They sing, laugh and show their emotions in everything they do. They know when a gringo is being open to them and**

treating them with respect, and they return the feelings they get from you.

Chapter 34
Exploring Baja and Beating the Heat

Today is September 1 and we have just returned to the Ranch after being gone for one week. We left on August 24 during a heat wave in which we found ourselves driving between El Centro and Brawley in 115-degree weather. This is 'cook an egg on the sidewalk' temperature. By Thursday we had finished all our errands and doctor visits. Dr. Madrid, my chiropractor at the clinic, finished cracking my neck and giving my body the needed adjustment so I could return to the volleyball net in the pool and practice in the ritual conducted daily at 12:30. Dr. Madrid turned out to be the best discovery I made in the clinic. His interest in the development and what is going on in the San Felipe area may entice him to come down for a visit in the near future. I would welcome a good bone-cracker living on the Ranch.

(2014 update) I have since made contact with a Dr. George McClellan who lives in Playa de Oro. He is a Chiropractor who comes down to the San Felipe area every three weeks and takes walk-ins at his house. Chirogm@hotmail.com

We headed west after our medical appointments to cool off in the 90-plus temperatures of Ramona where Suzanne's niece, Roxie, lives with her five Arabian horses, two dogs, three cats and two chickens. Roxie is an animal lover, as the reader should be able to tell. When visiting, we get to rest for a few days away from the Imperial Valley and Baja heat and give Roxie human companionship. Our cat, Kali, who lived with us in Arizona, now has a home with Roxie and all the other animals and seems to be adjusting rather well.

I have discovered a corner in the house where I can write in the mornings and drink coffee. I do this at our house on the Ranch. I go each morning to the porch facing the mountains. The difference between the two locations is the quiet. The neighbors in Ramona eventually wake up and drive off to work, but in the Baja house only a few cars can be heard as I gaze over the Sonora desert with ocotillo, palo verde and pipe cactus plants growing around the house. The local jackrabbit hops by our Mexico house in the morning as he heads towards the neighbor's home, unoccupied in the summer. He goes there to trim the many plants found in the backyard of the vacant house. Everything is fair game in this desert climate, and the only way to stop the wildlife from entering your yard is to own a yapping dog, which some people do, or build a ten-foot wall and eliminate the views of the sea and surrounding mountains.

Roxanne is always happy to see us and we become a welcome break in her busy schedule. She works near La Jolla Monday thru Thursday, and on Friday she stays home completing all her obligations on the computer. Feeding all the animal family members in the morning before going to work is just the beginning. She returns in the evening to repeat the same feeding task plus mucking out the stalls and working out a few of the horses before night sets in. This description of her life gives the reader the real picture of owning beautiful horses and caring for them on a miniature ranch.

Suzanne is always willing to cook a good healthy meal at night and I join in with clean-up. Roxie is able to sit, relax for an hour and visit with us before showering and going off to bed. She wakes with the rooster at sunrise to start the day all over again. Having family there is always nice, and on this trip we were able to give support. She had to be at home for the weekend and the first two days of the workweek nursing one of her horses back to health. The mare came down with a virus and a high temperature of 106-degrees. This particular horse was the mother of a newborn filly, and getting her healthy again was important for the milk production needed to feed the little one.

By Monday Suzanne was feeling better after having come down with a stomach problem when we arrived. I too did not want to do much after the high temperatures in El Centro and surrounding areas. We headed to the beach called Moon Light on the coast and had lunch with Michael, Suzanne's brother, before braving the cool Pacific Ocean, barely warm enough to swim in. Flash backs of growing up just down the road in La Jolla and surfing in 54 -degree water in the winter did not make it any easier for me to get totally wet in the 63-degree summer water temps.

The cool waters did not seem to bother the many bathers catching the waves with their Boogie Boards. The board surfers were further south of the bathers and all of these wave riders wore full wet suits throughout summer. When the surfers of the 60's braved the waves of summer, only a pair of swimming trunks completed our wardrobe. In the winter, wet suit tops were the only protection available to us, while our legs turned blue. We either got used to the cold water or we became fair-weather surfers. We were tough.

We returned to Ramon for one more night. The decision to go back to the Ranch through Tijuana and Ensenada was not a tough one to make. Staying near the Pacific coast and the cool temperatures instead of driving through the continued heat wave beating down upon the Imperial Valley and Mexicali introduced to us a new area of Baja. A few errands filled our morning as we picked up some items in the big box stores on the way to the border.

Neither of us had been to Tijuana for many years. When I was in college in the late 60's I went to Hussong's near Ensenada with some classmates from Santa Barbara. The bar is famous, established in 1892, and a must place to go to on a visit. The Ensenada Yacht Race, an event held each year, usually finds the winner of the water challenge coming into the bar with their trophy and continuing with the party atmosphere. An old high school friend even face booked me and wanted to know if the bar was still there. She said she spent a lot of time south of the border in her youth and had many stories to tell about her time spent in the establishment.

Crossing the border was completed without problems. The first thing we both noticed was how much the city had been cleaned up. I could see Tijuana was doing their best to change their image from what it used to be in the 60's and 70's into a modern Mexican city with clean streets, new storefronts and many big box and American chain stores open for business. The Golden Arches could also be seen as we continued onto the road directing us towards the coastal highway and Ensenada. Gas was our first needed stop and we had to take a side road to the small community right on the ocean in order to fill up. A few missed turns while winding our way back to the coastal highway gave us the side-street tour of the beach town and all it had to offer. We eventually found the right road towards Tijuana and the entrance to Highway One, which would take us all the way along the Pacific Ocean to our destination. Because we did not drive through the middle of Tijuana on this trip, I cannot give the reader a thorough description of the town other than what we saw crossing the border and driving towards the ocean.

Pacific Coast Developments: I have heard about the developments along the Pacific coast of Baja for the past twenty years. Americans and other foreigners were able to build beautiful homes on the Pacific Ocean for half the cost of a similar house in California. Twenty years later I have also heard the prices increased and the Mexican coast of Baja California has neared property prices of the California coastline. We did not stop in and check any of the real estate values but we both admired the beautiful homes and gated communities built on the ocean cliffs and hillsides with some of the most photographic coastline equal to anything I have seen along the California coast.

Coming around a bend in the road we found evidence of the Mexican religion and their steadfast faith in the Catholic Church. A huge statue of Jesus, with his arms outstretched as if he were blessing the community, stood on the hill overlooking the ocean and the homes below. All the houses were built in either Mediterranean or Southwest styles, and the colors of white, orange and yellow reflected the same choices of many of the homes found on the Ranch where we lived.

Statue of Jesus blessing the coast of Baja

Most of the coastal cliffs were filled with these community developments. More hillsides were being bulldozed and graded for future residents as we drove down the ocean highway. If any of the readers are thinking about a home in Baja and money are not an issue, now would be the time to shop the Pacific. The economy has lowered prices where we are living on the Sea of Cortez, and I am sure the same impact is changing the asking prices for real estate on the Pacific Coast. Stores and services were also seen on the drive south. The Mexican entrepreneur continued to find the needs of the foreign residents and filled them.

We arrived in Ensenada around 3:00 P.M. after passing through the north end of the city, where the fishermen from all the boats dotting the ocean brought the fruits of their labor. The smell was overwhelming to Suzanne, who has had an aversion to fish since childhood. She was able to hold her breath in two-minutes segments in order to stop from decorating the interior of the car with processed lunch. After five minutes we were past the worst part of the odor and continued on through the town looking for a suitable place to stay for the night.

A few side-trips through the busy city, which had tripled since my last visit over forty years ago, finally brought us to a suitable hotel in a modern part of the city. The hotel, named the Ensenada Inn, had a protected parking area inside a gate, and the hotel appeared to be clean and kept up to a high standard suitable for any American wanting a place to stay. The manager was friendly and respected my attempt to speak Spanish with him. A small pool in the yard and free Wi-Fi gave me everything I needed. Suzanne like the place as well and even put up with the hard bed, which seemed to be the norm in some of the places we have stayed throughout Mexico.

Ensenada Inn

The car parked next to us at the hotel had an El Dorado sticker, which meant the person was a resident of the Ranch. We knocked on the door and a German gentleman answered. With his limited English and my somewhat better ability to speak his language, we found out he had come over to the coast to escape the heat and explore the town on his bicycle during his mini-vacation. He did live on the Ranch but I did not write down his address. I will just have to bump into him at the store or post office some time and say hello again.

After dinner in a quaint restaurant-bar down the street, plus a shower upon our return, we ended up on the bed for the rest of the evening. I worked on my computer answering e-mails and Facebook messages from the past two days and Suzanne did crossword puzzles. Describing the coastal journey to my friends was necessary while the images were still fresh in my mind. The quiet location of the hotel allowed us to get the needed rest after the drive down the coast. We also obtained the directions to Federal Highway 3, the road over the mountains and back to San Felipe, so we were ready for the next adventure in Baja.

Morning came early for me. The hard bed did not allow a deep sleep. I greeted the sun, went to the office for morning coffee, and started to do a little writing about the visit in Ramona. So far I have been able to keep up with the documentation of our life in Mexico within a day or two of each experience. The office coffee was the strongest and best hotel coffee we have ever had either in Mexico or in the States. I went back for a second cup. On the way I tried to get a few words from the macaw parrot located in a large cage just outside the office. I said good morning to him in English as well as Spanish but could not break the language barrier of this tropical beauty. We packed, ate some cereal out of our empty coffee cups, and followed the directions to the highway.

Federal Highway 3 took us to the backside of Ensenada along the foothills, giving us a view of how the city had grown and filled in all the canyons and higher elevations surrounding the valley. The lack of street signs in Mexico meant the driver needed to trust the directions given or eventually pull over and ask at a Pemex station. I choose the latter. The attendant confirmed we were on the right road so we continued towards the back of the city and up the winding road taking us to a place we have never been before.

Travel Tip: Most of the residents at the Ranch emphasize the need for all driving in Mexico and other Latin American countries to be done in the day. I believe many Mexicans adhere to this rule as well. Night driving would be fine on the toll roads like the one we took from Tijuana to Ensenada, but the road we were on and other non-toll roads should be driven only during the daylight hours. If the day is getting late and you have many miles to go before reaching your destination, then find a comfortable hotel, eat a meal, and continue the journey in the morning. Cell phone coverage may not be available in isolated areas of the country and if car trouble happens, you may be sleeping in the back seat overnight before any help can be reached or any other cars come along and give assistance.

Federal Highway 3 was a road needing daylight to navigate. The twisty curves and steep embankments off the side of the pavement, with no metal rail protection to stop a car from going over the edge, marked a vast difference between the U.S. and Mexico. Mexico is doing their best to improve their main highways into the country, but there is no money for the car safety needs I have just described, especially on minor roads going over a mountain range. As we proceeded along the drive, Suzanne could not help but notice the many crosses marking the spots where fatalities had occurred in the past. Mexico is a religious country, and any deaths in the family are honored with remembrance markers, fresh plastic flowers and other symbols to honor the dead. After counting twenty such roadside tributes to the deceased, Suzanne stopped. By now I was gripping the wheel so tightly the circulation to my fingers was cut off. I needed to relax my death-squeeze and allow the blood to return to my hands as we continued to negotiate the curves up the mountain and through the rugged terrain.

We finally reached the pass summit and dropped into the valley we heard so much about from those who had driven the road before. As we descended into the vast agricultural farming community we were greeted by a rock painting of the Virgin Mary on the right side of the road. She was at least 8 ft. tall and seemed to be blessing us for having made the climb into the valley safely. I stopped to try and get a picture of the religious symbol but I found no place to turn around. Backing up with the oncoming traffic driving down the road created the possibility of adding another marker on the side of the highway with our names inscribed in bold letters. We decided to get a picture on our next trip.

Dropping into the valley from the pass high above gives the driver a panoramic view of this vast farming community. Grapes are a major crop grown in this area and since the date was the first of September, the fruit was getting close to completing its lifecycle. As we drove closer to the vineyards, we could see netting covering the many rows of vines in the attempt to keep the number of grapes eaten by the flocks of birds circling the vines to a minimum. A root plant like an onion or garlic seemed to be the other vegetation in production and since this crop grew underground, the birds did not interfere with this crop at all.

A small store and Pemex station was located on the valley floor. For anyone reading this book and thinking of taking this journey, there is fuel for both you and your car along the way. We had already fueled up in Ensenada, so the bathroom and a couple of bottles of water satisfied our needs at the time. Continuing on through the valley, we could see areas of what the land used to look like, because it was not cleared and plowed. Small scrub plants and high-desert vegetation grew in these undeveloped sections. Water seemed to be in abundance.

What I have noticed while looking out my window in El Dorado during the summer months is that thunderstorms dump a good amount of rainfall over the mountain valleys to the west of us. By the time the clouds reach the last row of hills bordering our development, the rain has been released and the desert remains in its standard state of being: hot and dry.

We drove through two more valley areas where farming took place and eventually started our descent into the climate of the Sonoran Desert along the Sea of Cortez. The road along this stretch reminded me of Highway 5 in 2005. It was full of potholes and needed a major overhaul, just as our road from Mexicali to San Felipe received starting in 2006. In the middle of the desert alongside the empty road filled with tire-destroying craters, a llantera, or tire store, was erected. It was built from desert trees and branches and covered with some type of vegetation. I am not sure the owner carried all the sizes of the many types of cars driving down the road. Any repairs done to Federal Highway 3 would cut into his business and he may have to move his operation to another location where the potholes rule the pavement. The main function of this llantera was to repair and patch any tires that could be saved.

The Sea of Cortez appeared on the horizon like a mirage in the desert. The blue strip of color above the desert vegetation was a welcome site as we neared the military check-point located where Highway 5 and 3 meet. We were given a brief inspection by the guard and his only comment in his limited English was, "Shopping in Ensenada?"

He could see the three extra-large bags of chips protruding out of the box of food items we purchased in San Diego.

"No," I answered. By now he was not interested in my attempt to try my Spanish with him explaining how we purchased the food in San Diego and not Ensenada.

A few more peeks into the car and the guard motioned with his arm for us to move on. Just as we were driving away, one of the other army guards tapped on my window and wanted some help with his English lesson. He was learning from a manual he held in his hand and wanted the meaning of a Spanish word in English. Suzanne and I both attempted to figure out the question he wanted answered but our limitations in each other's language restricted us and we soon gave up. I was impressed the soldier was attempting to learn another language. Being bilingual is helpful in Mexico and can lead to a better paying job in most types of businesses serving the needs of the many Non-Spanish-speaking tourists coming to this country.

The last twenty miles from the federal military check point to the Ranch went quickly. The time was 1:30 p.m. so the trip from Ensenada took three hours including the stops to use the bathroom at the small store and Pemex station just over the pass. Several other stops along the road in order to find bushes along Highway 3 were included in the travel time. The strong coffee served at the Ensenada Inn seemed to be cleaning out my system, along with the quantity of water one needs to drink while traveling and living in the warm Baja summer. The number of breaks needed to empty my bladder reached five.

Well Water: After a quick stop at the local Rancho Market for fruit and vegetables and collecting our mail for the past week, we were soon home under the AC. It took twenty minutes to unpack the car and put the food away. We gave a sigh of relief that the refrigerator did not malfunction while we were gone as it did after our last venture out of the Ranch. Suzanne did discover we had no water coming out of the tap and I knew the reason. When we left, the water level was low in the tank and I needed to call to have the cistern filled upon our return. Had I filled the tank before leaving we would not have the lack of water problem we now faced. The water in the lines flowed backward after a long period of non-use. The water in our lines must have done this. I needed to fill the tank right away. As I was checking the cistern to see how low the water level was, I heard the water pump start. Upon inspection of the pump I could see the pressure was at 0, indicating empty water lines. I unplugged the pump because there was no switch to turn it off.

If a homeowner has a water cistern, they need to spend the extra money getting a water pump, with an automatic off switch to avoid what just happened. If I had not unplugged the pump it might have burned itself up trying to get water through the system and into the house. Getting water back into the lines involves priming the pump. Water needs to be poured into the primer hole in the pump before plugging in the pump again.

The next morning Juan's water truck arrived just before 8:00 a.m. with a load of water. When I called him the night before I told him we were out of water, so he came to our house first. My neighbor, Ed, had given me Juan's business card. Juan probably learned his English by speaking to all the American customers he services on the Ranch. He spoke to me like we had known each other forever. He wore a colorful Mexican tourist shirt with decorative patterns, and he looked more like he was on vacation instead of delivering water to Ranch inhabitants. He said the next time, if I was leaving town and the water level in the cistern was low, all I needed to do was to call and give him our address. I could leave the money under a rock on top of the cistern. Keeping the water tank full would keep the water pressure for the pump up and water in the lines.

Water Gauge: I have discovered a device used by residents to shut off the pumps when the water is low. It is a bobbing device that floats on the surface of the cistern water and is attached to the off switch of the pump. When the water is low the device is now hanging above the water and sends an electric signal to the pump to shut off. It is not expensive and could save the owner the cost of replacing a water pump.

After Juan left, I called Oscar from Fix it Express and he told me over the phone how to prime the pump. I borrowed a plastic container from Ed next door and filled the primer hole with water and plugged in the pump. A blast of water came shooting out of a small valve on the side of the motor drenching me with water at fire-hose pressure. It felt good to cool off, and I watched the pressure gage start to rise. I thought the water shooting out of the pump was the primer water and it would soon stop.

After a minute passed and the water continued to blast from the pump. I knew something was wrong. I spotted a small black hose hanging from the motor and realized the line needed to go over the valve that was shooting a stream of water across the pump house and starting to knock off the paint on the opposite wall. After a few attempts to reattach the hose, while the water blasted out of the valve, I was finally successful. I watched the pressure gage climb up to 50 and then stop. A small leak in one of the hoses developed because earlier I had unscrewed the hose and removed the white tape found on the threads to prevent such leaks. I needed to stop the pump, re-tape the threads, hook up the hose and start the pump all over again. I completed the project, and we soon had water flowing into the house again. I was now a pump expert.

(Update 2013)
When a resident starts to receive water from a certain provider, it is good to also ask the neighbors from whom they get their water. There are three or four water businesses where we live at the present and there is a slight variance in the price for the same amount of water. The residents who have lived in the area where you move will know who has the best price.

The next day was Friday, and we used the morning to do laundry and catch up on e-mail using the Wi-FI at the laundromat. The machines only used quarters and I had remembered to purchase a roll of the coins while in the States a few days before. With the clothes now clean, we drove to the pool to cool off and have some lunch. Suzanne got to try out her new goggles in the pool while swimming a few laps. Her knee was still stopping her from walking and she was trying out a new form of exercise. She had not attempted swimming during the 19 years of our married life. The daily water volleyball game was happening as usual. For the last game I was able to play because someone had to leave before 2:30, which was the cut off time for this sport.

Yesterday was Saturday and being Labor Day weekend I expected the pool area to be quite full. Suzanne and I attended Rancho Market's 'two for one' breakfast promotion, bought a few fruit items and headed to the pool by 11:30. The pool area was packed. We had to park in the back parking lot, which is used for parking overflow. Upon entering the pool we found two chairs and a stand for our new shade umbrella purchased in Sam's Club on our last visit to San Diego. I tried to sign up to play water volleyball but over 42 people had already completed the 6 teams. I did not know this was a tournament weekend. I found out those who wanted to participate in the games needed to arrive at least 90 minutes before 12:30 to ensure a place on one of the teams. Five other people and I had not made the cut, so we were only able to swim and watch the tournament from the side of the pool.

Every seat and patio lounge chair was full. Several regular players who live in the area sat behind where we were sitting. I tried to engage them in conversation but it was obvious something had pissed them off. They were not interested in conversation. The tournament proceeded and I noticed neither of the two regulars joined any of the teams during the event. I believe they were also on the list of six people who did not arrive in time to make it on one of the teams. They were angry and probably felt they should have been given special treatment and spots for the tournament. Poor babies.

As I mentioned before, water volleyball is like a religion to many of the residents of the Ranch. Not being allowed to play on tournament day was like not being allowed to take Holy Communion on Easter Sunday. The two men stewed as they watched the weekend visitors, who had arrived early and had taken their spots, having fun hitting the ball around. Several men from the weekend crowd looked like ex- football players. One in particular was especially large, standing around 6 foot 5 inches in height and easily 350 pounds of weight. Most of the pounds had turned from muscle to fat due to his lack of training for the sport he had obviously played in the past. They were all having fun and even those of us who were not playing that day, except for the two brooding men sitting behind me, enjoyed watching the games and yelling our approval after a good spike or fantastic save was made in the waist-deep water.

The regular female player who advertised her 'good set' weeks before was also in the tournament, but she behaved herself and no gestures or comments were made. The regular players were on their best behavior for the tournament and for the holiday weekend population.

Today is Labor Day and we woke up to the refrigerator going out again. A call to Oscar describing to him how the icebox sends out sparks and shorts out whatever breaker it gets plugged into. The response, "I will send Jorge out soon."

Oscar thought the compressor was starting to die and causing the power surges. I needed to run to the Rancho Market to get hielo or ice, so we would not lose all our food before the refrigerator got fixed. I found out about a law in Mexico when getting the ice and a bottle of beer for the afternoon event with the neighbors. I could buy the ice, but no alcohol is sold before 10:00 a.m. I needed to return for the beer at a later time. After arriving home, the refrigerator was packed with ice to stop the loss of all our food. Oscar arrived a few minutes later. With inspection of the icebox he told me the repair cost could exceed the price of a new unit. We tried to call my rental agent, Henry, with the news but all calls went to voice mail. Henry lived close-by so I drove up to his house and passed on the information to him personally. He had returned the night before bringing 50 mattresses from the States for the orphanage and had turned off his phone in order to sleep in.

I explained the situation and told Henry that Oscar had a loaner refrigerator he could bring out right away so we would have refrigeration and not have to haul ice every three or four hours to the house. Henry said he would swing by after breakfast and check out the situation. He would try to call the owner of the house before making any money decisions. All this was happening on Labor Day. By the time a call was made to the owner, she could not be reached. Henry came by with his load of mattresses on the way to town and promised to try one more time to reach the owner. If no connection was made, then we should go ahead and pay for the rental, get it installed, and let the owner decide what she wanted to do regarding a new fridge.

Henry left for town to deliver the mattresses, and I returned to the typing of this story and letting the reader know about yet another adventure while living in Mexico.

Appliances: It is important to know about the appliances one puts into their house for survival. Cutting corners and buying second-hand stoves or refrigerators may not be the best thing to do. Both of these items are necessary for living, and they need to be in top working condition. The stove in our house was new and only needed new gas valves to get it to work correctly. The refrigerator was now on its third round of attempts to get it working correctly and there was still no end in sight. Other things could have happened to it as well as the compressor going out. The electrical board on the back of the unit could have been damaged. The list goes on.

If the reader is planning on purchasing all the needed items to use in a household, a trip to the nearest large Mexican town or city might be useful. Comparing the products found in the big box store such as Home Depot, Sam's Club, Wal-Mart and Costco is important. Mexicali, Tijuana and Ensenada have these stores. Compare prices, and if the same item is sold in the Mexican store, then buy it because you will not have to pay the tax of bringing in new appliances from the States. I have been told the stores may deliver the item and the warranty will be good for Mexico. The same warranty might not be good in Mexico for the same item purchased in the States. Check the warranty yourself if you buy in the States. Laws change here all the time.

Oscar arrived about an hour later with the loaner refrigerator. He was alone but he managed to get it off the truck and into place while I changed over the food items to the loaner. Since the loaner was working just before he brought it, the inside remained cool and we would not have to wait for several hours for the unit to cool down. Getting the loaner icebox in place was easy but removing the larger and heaver unit took a little ingenuity on the part of Oscar. Using straps and different pulling techniques he was able to maneuver the heavy appliance into the garage and complete the task. By now the high humidity was taking its toll on anyone working in the heat, and Oscar was now dripping wet in his shirt.

Both Suzanne and I thanked him for his prompt response and for again saving all our food items from sure 'death by heat'. He left to check on his other workers doing jobs around town and possibly replace his shirt, reduced to a wet washrag in the September humidity. After a quick mopping of the floor and a return to the store to purchase my post 10:00 a.m. beer, we found ourselves on the bed for a quick nap following a shower to remove the 83% humidity and sweat from our skins. By 4:00 we were all rested and at the neighbors to celebrate Labor Day with them and other residents in the area. We definitely deserved a party after this day.

Chapter 35
The Great Southern Cal Blackout

Today is September 9, 2011, two days before the tenth anniversary of this generation's Pearl Harbor. Most of the weather in Baja and the Imperial Valley has been going through a heat wave with temperatures higher than normal. 103 to 105 degrees has been the high and for this late in September, even the locals have said these temperatures are unusually high. Yesterday was a pool volleyball day for me. I have worshiped in the 'church of divine spiking' four times now and seem to have survived the twisting and turning of my body as it attempts to set or hit the ball. Beer and margaritas along with whatever food specials for the day make up the communal meal at the pool for many of the players. The exercise received during the game, is adequate and play in the water is a good way to stay cool.

After the game Suzanne and I headed home to rest up and prepare for the Thursday afternoon social at a home close to ours. This event is well attended even in the low-population summer months, and both of us look forward to seeing another one of the beautiful homes built on the Ranch. I was planning on bringing my camera and starting to record some of the pictures for the book so the reader could see how magnificent these Baja homes really are.

After a shower and a muscle relaxant, both Suzanne and I laid down around 3 p.m. During our down time we both changed our minds about the social and decided to stay home for the evening. We planned to try and make the trip into town the next morning to see the vehicles for the Baja 300 as they paraded on the malecon during the sign-ups for the newest race in town. The Baja 1000, 500 and 250 already existed and now a different number needed to be added to the list. All the races were big moneymakers for San Felipe and businesses, especially those housing and feeding the wild and crazy participants from the States. The hope was this race would also bring more needed dollars to the economy.

My personal impression of the race, based on the Mohawk haircuts, tattooed bodies and wild and crazy looks in the eyes of those coming down to drive in this event, is that this race could be the equivalent of the X games in car racing. Those who race or come to view this off-road sport appear to be in the same category as those skateboarders and bike enthusiasts risking life and limb in their particular X game event.

At 4:20 p.m. our routine for next eight hours changed significantly. The AC shut off and the fan stopped moving the air in the bedroom. The power was off. As we lay on the bed we both felt the outage would be short, based on the simple fact that all the other ones had been only minutes in length. An hour later I started to wonder if only our house was chosen to be without power. A short walk to the neighbor's house and I now knew the whole neighborhood was without juice to run the fans. Suzanne, our neighbor, said she has lived here for 5 years and only one other blackout had happened which lasted over one hour. Ed pulled up in the driveway. He had gone to the guard gate to get more news of how widespread the outage was.

"The whole town of San Felipe was out," was his report. "Probably one of the Baja 300 drivers crashed into a power pole while practicing on the course outside of town."

Ed usually had a theory of why things happen in the area, and a driver crashing into a utility pole was his explanation for the latest unknown mishap.

I let Ed and Suzanne know I may be going into town for some ice so I could pack the refrigerator and save our food from the constant heat the month of September still provided. My neighbors had some friends who ran their house on a generator. They lived in an electric section of the Ranch but the power lines were still not hooked up in their area. Right now only those residents owning a generator or running solar batteries for their fans and AC made up the population not affected by the blackout. A solar alternative started to look like a real winning backup solution at this moment.

Power Alternative: If you are planning on living in a third-world country and the electric systems have blackouts, a good idea is to have a generator in the garage for such situations. The power box is located in front of the house were we live. It has a plug-in socket. All that would be needed to get a house online again is an extension cord from the generator in the garage to the power box. Even a small unit to run the fans and keep the refrigerator working would be enough.

After two hours of no power, I decided to drive to Rancho Market for ice and cool drinks. When I arrived, the storage bin for the ice had plenty of the small bags left but the large bag bin was almost empty. The owner was selling ice and cold drinks in large quantities but the concerned look on his face told me he had lots to loose if power was not returned to his market soon.

"Do you have a back up generator?" I asked him. "No" was his reply.

The reason for his concern came from the reports coming in from those buying ice and drinks in his store. Rumors were stating that all of San Diego and Los Angeles was having a blackout and maybe the whole state of California was without power. I returned home, packed the refrigerator with ice, gave Suzanne a cold drink and went next door to give them the latest report. Minutes after my return to our house, the neighbors were off to stay with their friends who were surviving quite well on their generated power. We were all alone. We had friends, but we did not know them well enough to call and ask if we could come over for the evening and wait out the power outage.

Suzanne and I sat on our back porch in the shade and welcomed the warm wind coming off the Sea of Cortez. Any air movement was welcomed. The house was starting to warm up as the Mexican brick began its release of hot air it had captured during the day. By the time darkness fell, we had set up some candles, eaten our cold cantaloupe for dinner and prepared for the warm evening ahead. Water in a bowl was placed next to the bed, along with a washrag to wipe down our bodies during the 92-degree evening on the desert. We would survive.

Suzanne could not sleep and I was doing my best to catch a few moments in the needed state of rest. Two rounds of the game 'twenty-one questions' helped a little, but by 7:30 we knew we had to try and sleep before morning. At 9:00 Suzanne from next door was returning home from her cool evening with friends with a new report. She knocked at the door and said, "Just live with it. The power will be off until sometime tomorrow. "

Suzanne never sugar-coated facts and always told it like it was. Someone in Yuma had zapped the grid and caused a shutdown to much of Southern California. Baja felt the affects of the shutdown as well. Suzanne was going home, but she lived in a house with good insulation in the walls, so the temperatures would not reach what we were now experiencing in the house next to hers.

I returned to bed and continued my attempts to fall asleep, but to no avail. I would wipe my body down with the washrag, which gave me a few minutes of relief, but the heat returned and I knew sleep could not compete with high body temperatures.

During the night, the AC started up and the fan began to spin. It must have been around midnight. I got up and shut the window, hoping the room would cool quickly so we would have a few hours of sleep before the sun rose over the Sea of Cortez. Even with the cool air pumping into the room, it took me an hour to finally nod off. With only a few hours of sleep, we both knew our trip into town by 9 a.m. was canceled because heat and a body deprived of needed rest is not a good mix.

The news in Los Angeles at 6 a.m. treated the story as a minor setback. People in one part of the city who had no power had to drive to the parts of L.A. with power in order to eat in the restaurants still operating. The biggest inconvenience for the L.A. population was the parking and having to wait in line before entering the eatery of their choice. We lived in a desert climate and faced heat stroke and other forms of discomfort attached to survival. When the power goes out down here in the summer and you have no backup generator you are in deep 'doo, doo'.

September 10, 2011 and the race has begun. I am sitting on my porch where I can be found each morning from 6 a.m. until around 9 a.m. writing either about the day before or what we plan to do during the coming days ahead. At around 7 a.m. a large cloud of dust started to rise along the road bordering the Ranch. I believe the distance is around five miles from our house to where the race starts. After a few minutes the roar of engines reached us and I could actually see the route where the drivers in the first running of the Baja 300 were headed. The direction of the cars seemed to go west towards the first set of mountains and then turn north along the base of the foothills.

It is a timed race, so the start for each vehicle is staggered to allow plenty of space for each driver to drive without being blinded by the dust from the previous driver passing through. The roar of the engines can be heard echoing throughout the valley and if anyone thought they were going to sleep in today, they were mistaken. I may head over to the starting line later in the morning, but right now I am content with sitting on my porch, facing the mountains, drinking my coffee and observing the dust of the vehicles from a distance.

Winter Heating: I have decided to add an updated bit of information regarding a better way to heat your home in the winter. It is now December 15, 2011 and we just received our electric bill for the period of November 10 thru to December 10. The previous month the bill was 90 pesos or $7. We required no cooling in the day and the evenings were warm enough to not require a heat source to take the chill off the desert night. We woke to a 70-degree house and the temperatures remained in the mid-seventies throughout the day.

Starting in November, we began using several electric space heaters to warm the areas where we sat. I was either typing in the mornings or we entertained ourselves with HBO specials and movies at night. When the sunset, the chill of the desert began to pour into the Mexican brick home just as the heat did in the summer. No insulation means a hot house in the summer and a cold house in the winter. We used the space heaters, knowing the electric splits used for cooling the house also had the capacity to heat the house.

During the month of November, I had begun a quest to find a propane heater to place in the fireplace and attach to the gas line already put into place by the builders. The search included Home Depot in El Centro and Mexicali as well as a few other stores selling home- improvement items. Mexicali had sold out with the previous cold snap and El Centro had air regulations because they were located in California and could not sell propane heaters. They could order one for us but I needed one now.

On our return from getting glasses in Algodones near the California border and searching Home Depot, Sam's Club and Walmart in Mexicali for a heater, we again pulled up to the military stop about 20 miles from El Dorado Ranch. A pickup truck pulled up next to us with a load of boxes headed to San Felipe. The pictures on the boxes showed an item that look just like what I had been looking for during my fourteen-day search throughout northern Mexico and the Imperial Valley. Propane heaters were on their way to San Felipe and I could get one the next day by going to the address on the business card the storeowner gave me.

Entertainment for the cars waiting to cross the border from Algodones to the US

Arriving in town the next day at the heater store, I reminded the owner of our meeting at the military checkpoint. After a few minutes of attempting my basic Spanish and his basic English, I was introduced to the English-speaking employee who worked in the store. Every store who has gringo customers seems to have at least one of these people working for them and this store has theirs. The heaters that were brought in the night before were the newer models of a portable variety that could be moved from room to room. The propane bottle was strapped onto the heater and needed to be refilled every few weeks depending upon how much the person used the heat source. I told the man I wanted one that fit into the fireplace. He had two such models left, and they had been in his store since last year. I guess my search in

San Felipe had not covered enough ground, because what I was looking for was within ten miles of where I lived all the time. With the correct attachments and gas line for the stove, I was able to connect to gas heat the next day and warm up the house.

The electric bill for the month of November into December was $126, a jump of $119 from the month before. It seems the electric space heaters with the fans blowing out the limited heat to where you are sitting use a lot more energy than previously thought. The split coolers and heaters also use a lot of juice, and those who have been living down here for a while have switched to the Z gas alternative and have cut their heating bills. I have now made an estimated guess based on the amount of propane we have used since purchasing the heater, that our next month's electric bill will drop back to a low amount again like in October, and the propane usage could be around $50 instead of more than double the amount of yesterday's electric bill.

(Update 2013)
We are now living in another house and have purchased another propane heater that can be moved around the house on wheels. It cost a little more than the fireplace insert. Our electric

bill was 300 pesos during the months of December and January. We had to refill the propane bottles three times for a total cost of 360 pesos or around $30.

Chapter 36
They're Baaaack

For the past two days, September 10 and 11, the temperature has started to drop. The evenings are now in the 80's instead of the 90's and from what I have been told by the population living here for many years, this is the first indication of the shift in the weather and the return of the Snowbirds. From now on more residents who do not live in the area during the summer will be returning to the cooler temperatures of fall and warmer winters in Baja.

The Great Rain of 2011

September 13, 2011 was the day of the Great Rain. Since it was a Tuesday, I happened to be at the main building at the Ranch called the Pavilion. Most of the games like Mexican Train Dominoes and San Felipe Rummy are played there now and with the increasing number of residents returning, larger numbers of tables are needed. A small golf shop is located in the middle section of the building, with a restaurant in one wing and a large multi-use room in the southern section of the building. Seven or eight tables of domino players with six at a table made up the event for the afternoon.

Around 2 p.m. the first drops started to fall. No one thought much about it because we had had a small storm the afternoon before and only the hillside homes received any significant amount of rain. Those of us at the full moon gathering at the beach barely got wet. I believe it was around the time we played the nines when the storm started to get serious. Playing the nines would be understood if you played Mexican Train. If you move to Mexico or any other South American country or pick the game up at Toy R Us for around $18 and play, you will then know what I am talking about.

The wind started to pick up, and soon the patio was completely wet with large drops of water increasing every second. Golf carts could be seen coming off the course and heading to the golf shop. Along with the storm came lightning. Any golfer knows they can become a grounding conductor while at the apex of their back swing and become toast in a few seconds. The Ranch might have to rename the hole after the player who died from a lightning strike, or at least have one of those roadside crosses placed in their honor. No one would want such a special memorial. Instead of one of the nine Mexican artist or nine Revolutionaries who make up the eighteen holes on the course, a statue of the golfer just about to hit a drive with a lightning bolt coming down from the sky would be in place. Lightning striking his golf club would tell the story for that particular hole where death came in an instant. "He died doing what he loved best" would be the quote on the statue.

My wife, Suzanne, was at the swimming pool during the storm and reported to me what happened with the population there. I mentioned that no one with any sense would want to be remembered for dying because of a lighting strike. I forgot about the regular water volleyball players at the pool. They are a 'breed unto themselves.' They continued to play the game with rain and lighting strikes pouring down from the skies. Cheers would go up as the storm increased its fury. They seemed to be challenging Thor the thunder God and daring him to try and interfere with their daily ritual.

Any lighting strike hitting the pool meant there would be many crosses surrounding the swimming area or a metal plaque with all the names of those playing their last game of water volleyball mounted on an altar near the game site. There is no lifeguard on duty at the pool and in Mexico, if the players want to play and died while involved in the second most popular religion on the Ranch, then so be it. When death comes and you are doing what you love best what higher statement can you make for your beliefs?

Meanwhile back at the Mexican Dominoes game we were now playing the fives. The rain was coming down so hard that all the Mexican workers at the restaurant came over to the windows to see the performance that nature was putting on. Rain in a desert community is not a common occurrence and this storm was a 'doozie'. Hail came down and lighting strikes hit near the Pavilion. After living in Flagstaff for ten years I was used to such powerful storms. Most of the residents on the Ranch were from California, and this rainmaker had many of the long-term residents leaving their game tables to stand with the Mexican staff and bear witness to its fury.

Finally our game finished. We were the last to put away our dominoes and dash to the waiting cars in the pouring rain. I had put off washing the Blazer and planned on getting it cleaned at the border like I usually do while in line, but nature was doing the job for me. Suzanne waited for me in the car doing crossword puzzles. We needed to make a trip to the store for some soymilk and drive home in the tropical storm, which somehow made its way to the desert dumping a lot of moisture. San Felipe gets about 2 or 3 inches of rain each year. We may have picked up over half of our yearly rainfall in the three hours the storm poured onto our community.

We arrived home crossing a few washes carrying the overflow of rain down the hill towards the ocean. We have a four-wheel drive so we were feeling secure in our return to the house. When we entered through the garage door we discovered a residence with pools of water in the dining room by the front and back doors. Many drips were coming down from the ceiling. Either the house was not sealed properly or this rare storm became too much for this particular structure. We believe the owner cut too many corners building it. I know who the builder is and will not mention her in this book, but she is also one I will never use. A house should not leak, and this casa had drips coming down from the ceiling, air conditioning units and from the windows in every room.

By 5 p.m. the storm finally stopped. Three hours of torrid rain was more moisture than this area had seen in quite a while. We cleaned up the floors and got ready for our trip to El Centro the next day. After dinner we relaxed and went to bed by 9 p.m. We needed to get some sleep for the three-hour drive in the morning and hopefully get through on the road, which was still undergoing repairs. We had no idea if the rains washed out any of Highway 5 heading towards Mexicali.

Crossing the Border: The next day we were out of the house and on the road. By 10 a.m. we arrived at the newer east crossing with only four cars ahead of us. We were told Wednesday was the best day to cross, and arriving around 10 a.m. gave those who worked in California time to cross between 8 a.m. and 10 a.m. Now only a few shoppers were crossing and the lines were short. There is a radio station for the Imperial Valley giving information as to how much time it takes to cross at either the newer eastern border or the main international separation in Mexicali. If the reader does not have a Sentri pass and does not want a long wait then try the Wednesday around 10 a.m. approach. It has worked two times in a row, and I plan on making it my day to shop in El Centro until I get my Sentri pass and can cross quickly on any day of the week.

(Update 2013)
The border crossing still remains a mystery to me. The new border on the east side of Mexicali still remains a good bet on Wednesdays, but the earlier hour of 9 a.m. might be a better bet. Also many people are purchasing the passport license. The car line at the border is starting to be a long one as well. The Sentri pass is the best way to cross the border in a short amount of time.

Passport License; While in line behind the cars waiting to cross the border, we noticed a new line beside the Sentri line. It had something to do with a special passport license and there were no cars in the lane. Not until we were returning the next day did he hear more about it on the radio. The Imperial Valley rock and roll station mentioned the new pass drivers from the States could apply for and gave the web site for more information. *www.getyouhome.gov* is the computer site to visit and find out about this new pass. I plan to visit the site today and see if I qualify for the card instead of going through all the procedures of obtaining a Sentri pass.

Today is Monday, September 19, 2011 and the Mexican Independence holiday is over. The big storm was almost a week ago and the desert is already showing the results of the rain. Ocotillos are the thorny bush-type trees found throughout the landscape, and they are covered in green leaves all over their plant bodies. The large thorns covering the plants are very sharp, and if one of these bushes is watered regularly, then the leaves remain and a beautiful orange flower appears on the tip of the branches in the fall or early winter. The pipe cactus plants also have grown in size as they swell up with the captured water, filling their interior cells used to store the agua for the long periods of dry conditions. The desert is a beautiful landscape and when given a little of the needed liquid to exist, a transformation occurs like no other show on earth.

Today is September 21, 2011 and I am again on my west-facing porch watching the mountains change their appearance as clouds float above them casting shadows and allowing beams of light to break through in certain areas. The quiet of the morning is broken with the banging of repairs being done on a house two hundred meters towards the west. Residents are returning to the empty homes resting on the desert landscape surrounded by the green ocotillos and the changes the powerful rains have made to driveways and patio landscaping. Yard and house repair trucks can be seen driving up the roads leading to the many homes dotting our neighborhood. Repairing the leaky roofs damaged during the storm and filling in driveways now spread across the desert floor is keeping the local economy going strong.

Yesterday was Tuesday, the day I usually play Mexican Dominoes. Several new faces appeared at the Pavilion with the intent of participating in the event. I assumed these were the first of the Snowbirds to return to the now manageable temperatures gracing the San Felipe weather pattern. In another month the number of players could fill the dining room of the Pavilion and the event may have to move to the much larger convention room in the south end of the building.

Chapter 37
We Are Here for Now

This last chapter is being written at the same time the editing is taking place. I know there will be more to add as the population of the Ranch increases with the returning homeowners making their way south. This same migration is taking place in Arizona, New Mexico, Nevada,

Texas and Florida and throughout the country of Mexico. The mentioned areas are known for having milder winters with plenty of sunshine. It is our intent to join the migration to the north next summer from July 15 to September 15, thus avoiding the high humidity and heat of these two months. Several other residents have mentioned their intent to live during the extreme summer months in Ensenada, where it is rumored a small house or trailer can be rented for $400 a month, with a view of the Pacific Ocean from the front door. Suzanne and I would love to explore the same possibility for the month of August after visiting family in California and Oregon in the early month of summer.

Roof Maintenance: The date today is September 22 and in just the past week the traffic on our road leading to homes further up the valley has increased from two or three cars per hour to six. Banging and repair noises can be heard from several directions as neighbors seal rain-damaged roofs and make routine maintenance repairs to their homes. The hot sun demands structures in the area to have their flat roofs painted with a special elastic sealing product that fills in any cracks caused by the extreme temperatures of summer and occasional heavy rain. Every three years most of the homes receive a new exterior paint job and if the owner did not like the color of the house before, now is the time to choose another shade of a desert hue. I still recommend the lighter colors which tend to reflect light from the sun versus the heat-absorbing dark shades such as the house we live in at present.

Suzanne planned a picnic last night to celebrate the first day of autumn. She always has some kind of celebration for the seasons, and for the first time in many years we have not welcomed in the calendar change with our close friends, Pam and Scott Anderson. They are still living in Flagstaff and at the same time looking down the road and figuring out where they want to be when they retire. Scott is the friend who helped me take the first load of furniture to Mexico in May more than four months ago. After being here for the summer and thinking back about the move, it feels like we have been here for a year.

Summers in Baja can be hot and this past season was one of the warmest on record. I have thought about having a lot of t-shirts made up saying, 'I Survived a Summer in Baja' and seeing how the locals who stayed the season reacted by buying a shirt celebrating the past three months. Instead I have a lot on my plate just in the publishing of this book and getting the word out about Mexico and the truth about living in the country south of the States.

I have discovered the residents who do stay for the summer are a seasoned bunch. They have learned how to survive the heat and many of them do not play water volleyball. Several are artists and spend their mornings doing their craft before the peak heat of the day arrives. My neighbor, Suzanne, designs clay pots with ceramic tile decorations. Others take care of some of the homes surrounding their neighborhood by watering plants and doing other jobs for the empty homes of the Snowbirds, now returning for the next nine or ten months.

Henry, the person who is managing the house we rent, owns a cabinet business and seems to keep busy throughout the year. His wife, Charlotte, has a nice gift store and brings in items she has found in different craft shows in the States thus giving the residents different alternatives than those items found in the tourist sections of San Felipe.

A weekly Saturday market is held on the Ranch beginning in October and many of the Americans sell different items either from their labors of art or items not available in the area.

Many Mexican crafts people show up and sell to the Ranch population everything they would need in their Baja home. The best fruits and vegetables are available at the market and sell out very quickly because the Ranch population is now reaching high numbers. Good food is in demand.

One woman whom I met three years ago paints tiles and sells them to the many residents either building or remodeling their homes. The best set of tiles I have seen in her collection is the whole length of Baja California, complete with all the towns, landmarks and places to explore. This complete map of Baja on tiles would look great in a shower or mounted on a dining room wall, making a wonderful topic of conversation for guests visiting for dinner.

"Look Alice! Here is Santa Rosalie. That is the little town we visited last year on our drive to Cabo San Lucas. Wasn't that restaurant where we ate on the beach the most memorable place during the whole trip?"

I plan to start up my framing business I ran from the house during the years we lived in Flagstaff. I was a photographer and a member of the Artist co-op for five or six years, selling landscape prints and framed photographs. I also was a teacher in the Flagstaff school district. I taught myself how to frame art and still carried many of the tools needed to continue the service. I could give the residents a professionally finished product to hang on the walls of their homes in the San Felipe area.

Chapter 38
Why Did I Write This Book?

Today is Tuesday and being retired and living in a community in Mexico, I do have to check my computer to tell me what day it is. Suzanne is off to water aerobics with our neighbor, Jackie, a certified instructor, retired nurse and a black belt in some Japanese martial art. Jackie is my neighbor who asked the man delivering gas to our house when I first moved here using her best Spanish, "Where is the closest hardware store?"

I still get a good laugh from that incident, and at the same time I have gotten to know her and see why some Ranch occupants do not use Spanish when they speak to a Mexican. Some are shy about trying out their Spanish. Jackie is one of the many single women who have made the Ranch development their home. She worked hard all her life in the nursing field and moved to Mexico to live as well or better than she could have in any of the 50 States of America. With only a few exceptions, most of the people she meets either speak English or can understand enough English to provide her with what she needs. She built a beautiful home for 1/3 the cost if the same house had been built in Arizona or California. Her living expenses are also lower than what they would be back in the States. These numbers are more than likely true for many areas of Mexico where other Canadians, Americans and a few Brits have made their home. I have even met a few Europeans from Germany and Switzerland since the Snowbirds have returned. I better include Holland as well.

Choosing to write this book is mainly for the population of the States or any other western county in Europe who have considered retiring in a warm climate and want to live as well on their fixed retirement income as when they were working. The advantage of Mexico, Central and South America is that most of these countries are open to the development of communities or areas catering to the foreign resident. The biggest hurdle one has to make is the question they have to ask themselves: "Why would I move to another country to retire?"

My repeated answer to that question continues to be this: **Making such a move is not for everyone**.

I have covered many of the obstacles one faces, and I believe I have done so in as an unbiased way as I could. I do have my views and strong feelings regarding people who look down upon other cultures and make assumptions about other countries based on slanted news coverage and false statements. Limited thinking has always caused me to expose such narrow-mindedness whenever possible.

The stories were written within days of them happening so the facts could be remembered as I put them into the book. The community Suzanne and I moved to is also unique because of its proximity to California and Arizona. Family is important to us, so the distance to visit them is not as great as Costa Rica or someplace on the Pacific closer to Mazatlan or inland near Mexico City. Suzanne will be using Medicare next year and I am already on the system, so we have to be near the States to use the benefits.

The biggest stumbling block for many Americans who may be thinking about making a move is the comments from friends and the bias news coverage. News in the States seems to only touch on the drug wars carried on in the border regions of Texas, Arizona and one or two locations in California. The population in the states watching the news stories seems to think all of Mexico is a war zone and no one is safe. Nothing could be further from the truth.

Learning to Love the Peso is not an attempt to change anyone's mind about moving here. The point I hope to make is this: There is an alternative to working hard all your life, retiring and struggling to make ends meet in the later years. Most of those who have been living here for a while have come down many times before making the move. They have adjusted to the changes and enjoy the lifestyle of living in a beautiful home and having enough money from retirement and Social Security to still travel and remain active in their later years.

One person I know named Donita moved here after visiting for two weeks. She came from South Dakota. She sold her possessions she was not attached to and found a beautiful home to rent for around $500 a month. Her sister, Val, had been living here for many years and finally talked her into coming down for a visit. Val found the house and made the arrangements to rent it. Donita has been here since February 2011 and seems to have made the adjustment rather well. She has now been here for two and a half years and is in the process of buying a home in the solar area of the Ranch. (Update: She bought a house in the electric area and is presently settled in.)

A move such as the one we accomplished can be done because we and many other Yankee gringos have done it. Any interested persons thinking of a change in life, needs to make the journey to the area or community more than once. Question the residents and regarding the areas of concern I have written about during our move. Some of the individual needs may not get complete answers until you have made the transition and discovered the answers for yourself.

After you have made a few trips and have dispelled the myths about Mexico and the untruths stating it is dangerous, then stop asking your friends what they think about your possible relocation into a third-world country. Many people in the States simply have not visited Mexico other than a quick trip to Tijuana to get their car upholstered or a short walk to Algodones to buy prescription drugs, get new glasses or have some dental work done. They make the drive to this border town because they can no longer afford these services in the States because of their fixed incomes. Dental and medications are extra expenses on almost all health plans.

I get messages all the time from friends in the States who are sure I will be kidnapped and held for ransom. I have held off returning their e-mails until now. My answer to them is this:

"Poncho Villa and his gang have taken us hostage and demands 100,000 pesos by Friday. Can you round up some cash for us so we don't miss the bocce ball game on the beach? It starts around 5:00 p.m."

I usually do not hear any more horror stories from them and sometimes we do not get correspondence again at all. Many do not appreciate my sense of humor.

In the 70's during my nine-year journey around the world, I lived in or visited over 22 countries, staying longer periods in Greece, India, Holland and Australia. The cultures are different but I was able to adjust. The move to Mexico was not as much a stretch for me as it may have been for other inhabitants of the Ranch. Suzanne has not lived away from the States during her life and she has felt the challenge of making such a move. She also is adjusting and finding souls living here who share many of the same spiritual values she practices.

I hope I have made my point clear to the reader who may be interested in retiring or having a place to visit on vacation during the cooler months of the year. Many development communities provide tours to their locations in Mexico through the real estate companies handling the sales of property. Taking advantage of such a tour is a good beginning for getting a feeling of an area and seeing if such a lifestyle is for you. Once an area or community is visited and found suitable for your needs, return and visit the place on your own. Rentals are available for visitors and being by yourself without an agent giving you a tour is much more informative for you to discover if this is the right place to establish a residence. Some people know right away if the place they are visiting is right for them.

Do not be pressured into buying something you are not sure of. I purchased our property without Suzanne present because I felt it fit our needs as a place to visit each year and a possible place to live down the road. So far I feel fortunate that our plans have worked out. Trust your first impression and gut feelings about a location or community. If it is not the place for you, then visit somewhere else until you get the feeling you are home. Good luck and 'may the force be with you.'

Chapter 39
The Last Word

Today is October 20, 2011. Suzanne and I have just returned from Arizona from where we moved last June. Our close friends the Andersons, were in Phoenix, and I had not seen Scott since May when we made the big trailer move together. School has started again and there is a slight withdrawal I am going through after 25 years of teaching in California and Arizona. I will get over it. Teaching is a special job, and when several teachers get together there is never a lack of stories to tell about the years spent performing in this occupation.

I am again sitting on my porch and looking at the mountain ranges surrounding El Dorado Ranch just before sunrise. Suzanne has gone up to the roof to watch the sun come up as she does every day. Born and raised on the west coast, we always observed the sun setting over the Pacific Ocean but on the east coast of Baja the sun rises out of the Sea of Cortez. East coast residents would feel right at home with this act of nature.

As I sit on this porch after being gone for two weeks, the feeling of coming home has hit me for the first time. The quiet of the desert cannot be found in the city of Phoenix unless one lives on the outskirts of the noise and traffic. When I am here I am in a different world. This is a wonderful place to write and contemplate life and at 66 I have done a lot of that. I think I have found my place to live in the stillness.

For those wanting activity, that also is available in the many events described throughout the book. Golf is available and I have only touched on that sport because I do not play it. I have been told it is a decent course and played right on the shore of the Sea of Cortez. Off-road adventures can be found in this amazing desert, and those seeking that kind of fun will be satisfied.

The different organizations in town have also started up their recruitments for the new and old residents. Lions and Rotary clubs are two of the main organizations servicing the needs of others, along with many other groups handing out flyers to residents for this fundraiser and that potluck. Many of the different communities throughout

Mexico also have similar groups of people in service organizations, and a new resident only has to shop around. The Snowbirds are back and the winter activities have begun.

Yesterday was a special day for me. Suzanne went into town to teach her yoga class and called me about 9 a.m. On her return, she had a tire go flat, our second in a week. This was also the first time Suzanne had gone to San Felipe by herself. A flat tire and alone in San Felipe with limited Spanish and she had never lived in another country before. I told her to try and get it fixed at one of the many tire stores along the road. For the next hour I was a little concerned. Would this be too scary for her to go through?

She returned as if nothing had happened. She said the tire store fixed the tire in twenty minutes and it cost $5 or around 60 pesos to patch the wheel. She said she felt comfortable and driving alone is not a concern any longer. I believe we have made the final hurdle regarding our being here. Only four months ago Suzanne was wondering how she would ever adjust to being in Mexico as a vegetarian who does yoga and meditates each day. She now has several spiritual-minded friends with whom she reads the Course in Miracles each week. Mexico is a place that can be adapted to. Suzanne is in the minority in her eating habits but she is learning to adjust.

My final comment goes out to those wanting something different in their lives, either in retirement or for a break from the fast paced life of the Yankee gringo world. Each time I came down to San Felipe over the past six years, I would get a quick fix of the energy surrounding Mexico and its pace of life. Living here enables me to experience the 'mañana' mentality everyday. Morning sunrises are special in the desert as well as sunsets over the mountains, both experienced from the many rooftops on the Ranch in a celebration of life. We are both starting to love this place called Baja California. As we make the adjustments from the States and the pace of life up north, I now see why so many Europeans, Canadians and U.S. citizens call it home. The currency in Mexico is called the peso and as we continue to use the local monies instead of the dollar, I feel the shift is part of totally being here.

I cannot give the reader the feelings of living in another country by writing a book. The only way one can find out if Mexico or any country further south is right for you is to visit the area. You will know when you have found an area that fits your needs. This book is a guide with my stories about the move and setting up a home. My plan is to publish the story on e-book and continue to update the information as more is learned and as things change in this country. In Mexico and Latin America things are changing all the time.

Almost everyone I have met who lives here says they feel safer than in the States. I just met a young American couple yesterday. They moved to the Ranch last year and have two children in the local schools. The gift of learning two languages and experiencing another culture is the best education the parents can give to their children. They also say they feel safe having their children in the schools and walking around town by themselves.

Today is Dec. 2, 2011. The Spanish lessons I attempt to listen to each day by Michel Thomas have helped me overcome the communication problems I may have faced if I made no attempt to learn the language. Suzanne continues her lessons in San Felipe and loves the fun way of learning the language. I sell photography in the weekly market on the Ranch where I live and frame other people's art they have purchased in Mexico. The final copies of the first edition hardback cover of *Living Beneath the Radar* are also selling quite well down here. It seems others living here want to read a good travel story and the book fits their needs.

Suzanne and her Spanish class in San Felipe

I have even written a third book *Centavo, A Dog from Mexico*, based on the true story of a street dog being adopted by two gringos from Flagstaff, Arizona. The story is from Centavo's perspective and describes all the adjustments and transitions she has to make from being a dog on the streets of a Mexican village to the home and lifestyle of a family in the States. The creative juices really seem to flow down here and I am taking advantage of the moment.

(2014 update) *The 60's; If You Remember It You Didn't Live It* is also finished and self-published through Create Space on Amazon. Most of the inhabitants down here are from that period in American history. If they want to read about what many do not remember, then here it is.

I also have finished the first draft of *Between a Rock and a Blood Clot*. The story is my first attempt at writing a fiction mystery and was done with my wife, Suzanne. It should be available early in 2014. Few distractions lead to creativity.

A cold snap started on December 1st and the moisture and cloudy days have dropped the day temps to the 60's. I woke up to 57 degrees this morning but still remember living in Flagstaff in the winter where the high for the day may not reach 50 degrees. I loved that Arizona town but the winters are no longer something I care to live in anymore. Temperatures in the 60's and sometimes in the 70's throughout the winter is a much more desirable climate for us.

Today is January 23. We are moving from this house of Mexican brick and no insulation. For the past eight months we have been living in a house not built to the standards of being suitable for a full-time resident. If we only rented this house during the months of October, November, March, April and May we would be fine. The daughter of the owner came by after we told the owner we were moving and could not live in a house not insulated from the cold and the heat. She tried to tell me all the houses in Baja were built that way and to expect $300 to $400 electric bills in the summer.

Do not believe such a fabrication from anyone if you are looking to buy or build in Mexico. An insulated house will not have high electric bills and will cost much less to cool in the summer and heat in the winter. Find out what the house is made of before you buy or rent. Cutting corners in construction and not having the best R factor possible will cost you in the long run. Double-pane windows and shades for the glass are also a must for the summer. Insulate first and spend money on decorations last. You will thank me later.

Santa Claus lives in Baja after Christmas. He plays Mexican Train Dominoes at the Ranch with other residents.

Presenting the truth about Mexico, and not the country portrayed in the American news is my intention. The country is not a war zone, and what it offers to those who live here is an opportunity to live well on retirement income near a friendly town called San Felipe in a community we call home. Come on down for a visit. Life is good and we are enjoying it down here. This is how Suzanne and I are *Learning to Love the Peso.*

About the Author

The author lives in Baja, California near a small town call San Felipe on the Sea of Cortez. He moved there with his wife, Suzanne, in 2011 after retiring from a teaching career in Special Education in 2008. He is the author of four books including ***Living Beneath the Radar; A Nine Year Journey Around the World, Learning to Love the Peso; How to Move to Mexico and Why, Centavo; A Dog From Mexico, The 60's; If You Remember it You Didn't Live it.*** He continues to live in Baja writing and living a pace of life suitable for the creative mind. His web site is **www.JeffreyRCrimmel.com** and he can be reached through his e-mail at the site.

Author reading his Kindle on the beach in Baja, Mexico

Additional Photographs
Showing the many changes to San Felipe

Water Volleyball, February, 2012. (old pool)

New pool.   May, 2013 with Water Volleyball court.

The new lap-pool is one of three new pools in the complex.

The malecon was re-done in 2012-2013 and is beautiful.

New Mexican grocery store located in San Felipe.

There are plenty of vegetables to eat in the produce section.

Parrot's Cracker is one of the new restaurants located near the Ranch. 2013 Photo by Linie Sherrod

Fishing boats along the malecon. 2010

New 7-11 built on the malecon in 2013
Photo by Susan Woolsey

The new casino was finished in 2013. No need to travel to the States to lose your money. You can do it in San Felipe.
Photo by Cliff Russell

Dancers at Shrimp Festival in San Felipe, 2011

Singers at Christmas 2013

My neighbor, Ed, from the first house we lived in.
He is walking his dogs the easy way in Baja.
2011

The Road Runner moved to their new location.
Business has done very well.
Peso book is also flying off the shelves. Thanks
2013

One last shot before we say good-by from Baja

Thank you

I would like to thank Marge Scott. After my first two readers, Rebecca and Ed, gave me their corrections, she read the book and handed me 55 pages of more changes needed. All three live on the Ranch where I live. I appreciate any help in this area of editing. I would recommend Marge for anyone writing a book. She is a thorough proofreader.

Glossary of Information

A
Appliance Information
Pg. 205, 346

Air Conditioning
Pg. 189

Adjusting to Mexico
Pg. 222

August Heat
Pg. 201

American Cell Phones
Pg. 210

B
Bathrooms
Pg. 27

Building Information
Pg. 177, 274

Border Crossing
Pg. 182, 365

Banking
Pg. 229

C
Cell Phones
Pg. 209

Customer Service
Pg. 251

D
Dental and Medical Tip
Pg. 195, 276, 315, (chiropractor)

Dateland
Pg. 106

Driving in Baja
Pg. 45

E

F
Fourteenth Amendment of the U.S.
Pg. 76

Furniture Tip
Pg. 85

Food Tip
Pg. 223

FM Information
Pg. 230

Fideicomiso
Pg. 278

G
General Observation
Pg. 254

Gasoline
Pg. 156

H
House Building
Pg. 263

I
Information and News
Pg. 167

Internet Information
Pg. 167

J

K

L
Language
Pg. 161

M
Mexican Hotels
Pg. 33

Medications & Medical Info
Pg. 81, 195, 275

Moving
Pg. 95, 124, 186

Mexican House Information
Pg. 187

Mail
Pg. 226

Mexican Dominoes
Pg. 235

Money Exchange
Pg. 251

Mexican Brick
Pg. 273

N

O
One Task a Day
Pg. 162

One Day at a Time
Pg. 239

P
Power Alternative
Pg. 351

Passport License
Pg. 285, 366

Pacific Coast Developments
Pg. 326

Q
Ask Questions
Pg. 310

R
Rooftop Information
Pg. 172, 369

The Great Rain of 2011
Pg. 360

S
Snowbirds
Pg. 57

S.A.F.E.
Pg. 125

Self -doubt
Pg. 190

Summer Heat
Pg. 201

Steve Forman
Pg. 240

Sentri Pass
Pg. 284

T
Translator Fee
Pg. 137

Tires
Pg. 146

Travel Tip for Mexico
Pg. 291, 332

Third-World Attitudes
Pg. 319

U

V
Visa information
Pg. 93

W
Water
Pg. 211

Well Water Info
Pg. 337

Water Gauge
Pg. 339

Winter Heating
Pg. 356

XYZ
Z Gas
Pg. 157, 159

Works Cited

Snowbirds: en.wikipedia.org/wiki/Snowbird

Fideicomiso: www.parkstrong.com   (playa de oro)

Sentri Pass: www.cbp.gov

Passport Card:
en.wikipedia.org/wiki/passport_card

www.ingramcontent.com/pod-product-compliance
Lightning Source LLC
Chambersburg PA
CBHW051812090426
42736CB00011B/1437